Praise for *Fire Up Innovation*

"Helene Cahen, equipped with her many years of experience in corporate environment, building her own business, and lecturing on innovation in leading universities, has come up with a practical book for all leaders to move their team to the path of innovation. Moving away from grand theories, this book provides a systematic and pragmatic approach built upon proven tools. Each chapter can be revisited on its own right to unblock a team onto the path of innovation. And the clarity on when to use which technique will save time and frustration."

Corinne Dive-Reclus
Global Head of Roche Digital Diagnostics
Advisory Board Member for Innosuisse
Mentor for the European Women Leadership Program

"The risk of not changing is greater than the risk of changing. This is what Helene Cahen's book Fire Up Innovation teaches us. In a concise and clear manner interspersed with practical exercises, this book lays out the core principles of innovation that will allow us to navigate and be more comfortable in our ever-changing world—whether as a team builder in a major corporation or as an ordinary citizen."

Hélène Mialet
Professor Department of Science Technology Society, York University Canada
Author, *Hawking Incorporated*

"Well written and engaging, it's a foundational read for those seeking to better understand how to cultivate a culture of innovation in today's constantly changing environment."

Yali Lincroft
Policy Advocate/Philanthropist

FIRE UP
INNOVATION

*Sparking and Sustaining
Innovation Teams*

HELENE CAHEN

Names: Cahen, Helene, author.

Title: Fire up innovation : sparking and sustaining innovation teams / Helene Cahen.

Description: [Berkeley, California] : [Strategic Insights Press], [2023] | Includes bibliographical references.

Identifiers: ISBN: 979-8-9889955-0-0 (paperback) | 979-8-9889955-1-7 (eBook)

Subjects: LCSH: Creative ability in business. | Teams in the workplace. | Creative ability. | Creative thinking. | Diversity in the workplace. | Artificial intelligence--Industrial applications. | Industrial management. | Organizational effectiveness. | Psychology, Industrial. | Personnel management.

Classification: LCC: HD53 .C35 2023 | DDC: 658.4/063--dc23

To my dad, a brilliant pharmacologist, who instilled my interest in innovation. And to my mom, a fierce and independent woman who encouraged me to create my own path and think outside the box.

Table of Contents

> **The potential power of creative imagination is all but limitless.** [1]

– Alex Osborn

[1]Osborn, A. F. (1963). *Applied Imagination: Principles and procedures of creative problem solving* (3rd Rev. ed.). Charles Scribner's Sons, 1.

Intention: *Sparking Innovation Through a New Lens*

This is not your regular, ordinary book on innovation. Or on anything in general. This book is designed to be interactive and experiential. It's not a book to read once and put aside.

Of course, you could do that, but you would miss the point entirely. Innovation and change are not concepts you can simply grasp by reading a book. They require you to try and do things differently.

My hope is that this book becomes a guide to support a journey of learning and a practice of new thinking and risk taking. Use it as a guide that you pick up and use whenever you travel in the innovation world. It will provide you the keys to a self-guided journey to understanding your own creativity and developing your innovation techniques, language, and tools to collaborate and innovate with others more easily and successfully.

I will leave you with this quote from French author Paul Valery which is engraved at the top of the Palais de Chaillot in Paris:

Il dépend de celui qui passe	*It depends on those who pass*
Que je sois tombe ou trésor	*Whether I am a tomb or treasure*
Que je parle ou me taise	*Whether I speak or am silent*
Ceci ne tient qu'à toi.	*The choice is yours alone.*
Ami, n'entre pas sans désir.[2]	*Friend, do not enter without desire.*

Hope you enjoy the journey. Bon Voyage!

◼ Why Is This Important?

We're at a time of great change. These past few years have shown us that, whether we want it or not, the world is changing, and we can't avoid it. As Anjali Sud, the CEO of Vimeo, said in a recent TED Women interview, "The only constant is change."[3] And the AI revolution is only going to increase the pace of change, with positive and negative impact being amplified quickly.

After COVID-19, many of us have likely reconsidered our personal priorities, evaluated whether our personal and work life are fulfilling, and are looking for new paths for ourselves and our organizations. We want to be satisfied in our work, and to find time and energy for our personal life. Organizations want to retain employees and find new and effective ways of working, while dealing with external changes that require fast adaptation.

To create change, to adapt, and to innovate in organizations is likely to require teamwork. AI is becoming more important to help with many tasks, but as of now and for a few years, it is likely that decisions will still be made by humans, and in the case of innovation, by teams. Typically, teams are brought together because of their experiences, functional expertise, and background. Yet, they often don't have formal understanding and knowledge of how to work together in a team, particularly in high-stake situations like innovation.

My expertise is in developing innovation teams, and I've seen firsthand how these teams often lack a common process, tools, and language to be able to work together effectively.

---

[2] http://clg-beaumarchais.scola.ac-paris.fr/CHAILLOT/inscriptions.htm.
[3] Sud, A. (2022). Anjali Sud and Stephanie Mehta interview. *How great leaders take on uncertainty* [Video]. TED.
 https://www.ted.com/talks/anjali_sud_and_stephanie_mehta_how_great_leaders_take_on_uncertainty?language=en.

This often starts with teams not being aware of their diversity of thinking, which is *the difference in how we each think.*

> **My expertise is in developing innovation teams and I've seen firsthand how these teams often lack a common process, tools, and language to be able to work together effectively.**

This book will begin by explaining our unique ways of thinking and solving problems, then address how teams operate, and finally provide practical frameworks and tools that can enhance teamwork. My hope is that this book will help make the invisible visible and the implicit explicit, so that by becoming aware of how we think and how others think, the work becomes easier, more effective, more collaborative, and, ultimately, more fulfilling and joyful.

As we will address later in this book, research by Casimer DeCusatis shows that teams aware of their thinking preferences "can lead to self-awareness of a team's relative strengths and weaknesses, and provide opportunities to balance the team membership to increase the prospects for long term success."[4]

As humans, we work with others to solve problems. Teams are everywhere. While many of the examples here are taken from the work world, the application of this book is also relevant when interacting with your family, friends, communities, and in nonprofit and educational settings.

---

[4]DeCusatis, C. (2008). Creating, Growing and Sustaining Efficient Innovation Teams. *Creativity and Innovation Management*, 17(2), 155–164.

Helene's Story

I've always been fascinated by creativity and innovation. Looking back at my journey, this has always been at the core of my work.

After business school, I looked for the most creative job I could get with my background. I started my career in advertising, first working in France with new product packaged good launches for Fortune 500 clients like Unilever and Nestle. Then, I moved to the US and worked at The Clorox Company in a customer insights role, where my focus was to understand customer attitudes, behaviors, needs, and wants.

In the early 2000s, I went back to school to get a master's in science degree in creativity and change leadership from SUNY Buffalo. There I found my tribe in the creativity world. I feel at home with people who are passionate about helping others access their creative potential and solve meaningful challenges. This graduate program gave me a research-based framework to understand the creative process, and I learned how to facilitate and support others' ability to reach their potential. I came to understand that while we are all creative, our individual thinking processes are somewhat unique.

Over the last two decades, I've worked with diverse companies from Fortune 500 organizations to small consulting firms, from tech firms to packaged goods providers, from fashion to health care, from startups to nonprofits. Regardless of their focus, this understanding and approach made a difference.

Writing this book is a way to share my 20+ years of experience and knowledge as a practitioner and "fire up" innovation leaders and teams, and give my readers a chance to learn and practice—wherever they are in the world.

■ Why It's Time for This Book

Through my work with teams, I've discovered that although you can find many tools for innovation in books or videos or AI, these tools aren't very useful without the knowledge of how they are best used.

You need context. Having a hammer isn't helpful if you don't know how to use it—or if you use it for everything—because it's the only tool you understand. You need to understand how to build a house and know which tools to use for which tasks before you start filling your toolbox.

I help people understand how to build houses.

Then I teach them which tools to use. I keep this as simple as possible, because more tools aren't necessarily better. The world doesn't need another tool book. We need more diverse builders and architects and contractors to bring the changes needed. And to understand each other. To do this, we need to be aware of the importance of diversity of thinking.

Our challenges—whether individual, business-focused, or collective world problems—are complex. Solving them requires diverse skills and thinking, but also a common understanding of thinking processes. Otherwise, we can't communicate well. We need to include diverse people in our teams so we can collaborate better across the board.

■ What You Should Expect in This Book

This book is meant to help you learn by doing—not by reading. That's why I've included examples and exercises you can do in your personal or professional environment. As you go through the book, you'll improve your understanding of yourself and others, and learn how to work better with others. And, if you're up to it, you can take the five-week challenge outlined in Chapter 9 to anchor and deepen your learning.

You may get the most from this book if you take the time to complete the exercises. Notice how they change the way you think. You'll also begin to start thinking about how *others think* in a broader way by observing, experimenting, and reflecting. While this book is ultimately about working in teams, you will notice that the exercises start with yourself, then add a partner, and then extend to your team. You may want to learn about yourself first, then extend to others, because by explaining to others, you're much more likely to retain more of the concept. This book is designed to work at the individual and team levels. I encourage you to do the exercises and apply the learning to your work and to your life. Then, discuss with others what you've learned and how they can also use these approaches.

That said, it's really about creating your journey. There are many ways to do this. Decide with whom you'll do the exercises, who to ask for feedback, and who you'll choose to share reflections.

◼ How to Navigate the Book

- While there's a natural order of learning in the way the book is organized, you can also choose your own adventure and read and do the practices in a different order or find a tool that you need for a specific challenge. I would, however, recommend reading and completing all the practice exercises before taking on the five-week challenge.

- Each chapter contains readings, practical tips, and at least one practice exercise.

- Also, if you want to have the exercises in one place, as well as a place to reflect and journal, you can download your Practice Journal and your 5-Week Challenge Journal using the QR code below.

- I recommend you complete the exercises by hand in the book, the printout, or your own journal. This allows you to access different parts of your brain and possibly to draw, in addition to just writing words.

Use this QR code to download a journal with all the practices in the book so you can write in your answers.

Pre-Journey Assessment:
What is your biggest challenge?

Let's start with a quick baseline quiz. Answer as quickly as possible, without trying to censor or filter your responses.

My biggest challenge right now is _____

I feel stuck _____

I wish I had a magic wand that _____

So I could feel _____

What I need to help me think through this challenge is _____

_____

This is how I'm planning to solve this challenge _____

_____

Here are the tools I already have available to me _____

_____

I'm going to ask you to do this again at the end of the book, after you've learned about frameworks, techniques, and tools, so you can reflect on your learnings and the impact of your journey.

Your Innovation Journey

Intention **Sparking Innovation Through a New Lens**	Chapter 1 **Illuminating Our Minds** *Shining a Light on the Invisible*	Chapter 2 **Igniting the Innovation Engine** *Understanding the Innovation Process*	Chapter 3 **Diversity** *The Fuel for Powerful Innovation*	Chapter 4 **Gathering Around the Fire** *Supporting Collaborative Diverse Teams*
Why Is This Important?	Another Side to Diversity	A Quick Background about Creativity and Innovation	Why Diversity Is So Critical to Innovation	The Importance of Empathy
Helene's Story	The Core of Creativity	Innovation Takes Many Forms	Blowing Up Silo Thinking	The Performance Team Equation
Why It's Time for This Book	Practice #1: Solve a Challenge Quickly	Thinking Practically about Innovation	Making Diverse Thinking Visible	How to Make This Equation Successful
What You Should Expect in This Book		Practice #2: Embracing Failure	Practice #3: Observing Diversity and Its Impact in Meetings	Practice #4: Meeting Management
How to Navigate the Book				
Pre-Journey Assessment				

Chapter 5 **Building a Fire That Lasts** *Principles of Applied Innovation*	Chapter 6 **Sustaining the Warmth** *The Basic Toolbox*	Chapter 7 **Lighting the Path** *Sustaining Creativity and Innovation*	Chapter 8 **Fanning the Flames** *Where Do We Go From Here?*	Chapter 9 **Getting Fired Up** *The Five-Week Innovation Challenge*
The Four Key Building Blocks	Tools for Clarification	A Virtual, Hybrid World Create New Challenges	Key Points Review	Week 1 You
Practice #5: New Ideas	Practice #7: Ethnographic Research	A Virtual/ Hybrid World Also Offers New and Sometimes Better Solutions	How to take this further? We can help	Week 2 You and another person
Practice #6: Create Your Own Learning	Practice #8: Generating Problem Statements			
	Tools for Ideation	Practice #11: Managing Hybrid Meetings	Practice #13: Post Journey Assessment	Week 3 You and the team
Guidelines for Diverging and Converging	Practice #9: Brainstorming	The Big Question: How Will AI Impact Our Thinking and Work Around Innovation, Creativity, and Change?		Week 4 You and those you can impact
	Tools for Developing Options			Week 5 Putting it all together
	Practice #10: Action Plan	Practice #12: Take a Challenge Through AI		

Chapter 1

Illuminating Our Minds: *Shining a Light on the Invisible*

Diversity, equity, and inclusion (DEI) in the Western culture is emerging as an important set of topics. It's often based on our moral sense of fairness, justice, and history, yet the subject has been politicized, which makes it challenging to apply and leads to slow progress. There are many experts and books written about the subject of DEI. We are not going to revisit their work. Instead, we want to talk about the importance of diversity in innovation and, in particular, bring a new facet of diversity that is not often discussed—*diversity of thinking*.

For the purpose of this book, we will define thinking as it relates to solving problems, and diversity of thinking as the different mental steps we may use to solve them. For instance, if I give you $200 for your holiday shopping and 30 minutes to spend it, how would you go about this? How would others do it? Check the practice #1 exercise at the end of the chapter if you want to practice more and reflect.

At a practical level in organizations, we know that diverse teams perform better, are faster, and that they positively affect the bottom line.[5] Helwett, Marshall, and Shelbin (2013) reported that research done with 1,800 professionals showed that companies with 2D diversity (that is with leaders that are diverse both inherently—on elements such as ethnicity, gender, sexual orientation—and in an acquired way, such as having lived abroad and developing an understanding for cultural differences) outperformed companies whose leaders are not 2D diverse: ". . . 45% are likelier to report a growth in market share over the previous year and 70% likelier to report that the firm captured a new market."[6]

■ Another Side to Diversity

Internal organizational problems, as well as client/user focused challenges that cut across different areas of an organization, are becoming more frequent and more complex. Each team member brings their own experiences and biases. So, a diverse group that might include representatives from different genders, races, backgrounds, types of life experiences, and organizational functions—as well as people who think differently—may be required to deal with complexity.

For some situations, group members with similar thinking might be fine. But to solve messy, poorly defined, or multifaceted problems, diversity of thinking is important. Let's say we have a group that is great at getting things done and jumping into action. This may be very useful, but it might be an issue if the group makes assumptions without taking the time to ensure they're working on the right problem, or considered alternatives before selecting a solution.

> **Diverse teams perform better, are faster, and that they positively affect the bottom line.**

This topic is rarely discussed, yet it's critical. It's not about recruiting people that think in a specific way or discriminating on the basis of how people approach problems, but learning to value and appreciate diverse thinking and to respect that people think differently.

---

[5]Lorenzo, R. & Reeves, M. (2018) How and Where Diversity drives financial performance. *Harvard Business Review*; Reynolds, A. & Lewis, D. (2017) Teams solve problems faster when they're more cognitively diverse. *Harvard Business Review*. https://hbr.org/2017/03/teams-solve-problems-faster-when-theyre-more-cognitively-diverse?autocomplete=true; Rock, D. H., & Grand. (2016). Why diverse teams are smarter. Harvard Business Review. https://hbr.org/2016/11/why-diverse-teams-are-smarter.
[6]Helwett, S.A, Marshall M. & Shelbin R. (2013). How Diversity can Drive Innovation. *Harvard Business Review,* December.

When we learn about differences in thinking, we can embrace the uniqueness of each individual and learn to work better and more constructively with others who think differently. It's important that people feel appreciated and seen for what they can bring to a team—rather than feeling rejected or unappreciated because they think in different ways. Remember the kids that were labeled disruptive, annoying, or creative when you grew up? It's likely that, to some extent, this was because of the teacher's own biases toward appreciating students who thought like them, which resulted in frustration with those who thought and behaved differently. A research study with 275 teachers showed that teachers *do* have a bias towards students who think the way they do, and they encourage or discourage qualities based on their own preferences.[7]

We often tell people they're not creative because we tend to define creativity narrowly—meaning only artists are creative, the same way we traditionally think only designers can design.

> **And yet, we're all creative and we're all designers, as we go through life solving problems and designing life solutions.**

When people are told they're *not* creative, they shut down that aspect of themselves and limit the opportunity to reach their potential. A hundred years ago, left-handed people were told they had to use their right hand to write. Even if they were able to do so, this limited their full ability to write comfortably.

Our existing systems limit our ability to reach our creative potential in terms of thinking broadly and solving problems. Sir Ken Robinson's TED talk on creativity, which has gotten almost 72 million views, has an interesting take on this topic. Sir Ken challenges us to think about the ways schools actually may be killing creativity by overfocusing on mathematics and language and putting art last. This focus is the result of the industrial revolution, where intellectual skills were highly valued to help support the system[8] and we needed

---

[7]Gurak-Ozdemir, S., Acar, S., Puccio, G., & Wright, C. (2019). Why Do Teachers Connect Better With Some Students Than Others? Exploring the Influence of Teachers' Creative-Thinking Preferences. *Gifted and Talented International*, Nov 2019, 9.

[8]Robinson, K. (2006). *Do schools kill creativity?* [Video]. TED. https://www.ted.com/talks/sir_ken_robinson_do_schools_kill_creativity/transcript.

standardization. Yet, we still have the same prioritization two centuries later in a transformed world.

Young children live in a world where they access their creativity to solve real or imaginary problems all the time. But in school, we're taught that problems have right and wrong answers. Think about standardized tests and the ways students are evaluated, particularly in the American system. It's all about A, B, C, or D. There are four answers: one is right, the others are wrong.

In the real world, however, we deal with more complex problems without a simple answer. In fact, we often have to start with little or no idea about what the solution may be. Because we're still trained to think there should be *one answer*, we worry about what will happen if we make the "wrong" choice.

If you were to ask preschoolers if they're creative, almost all of them will raise their hand (I did this experiment in my son's classroom when he was five). When I now ask this question to the teams with whom I work, only between 30% and 50% of hands are raised. And these groups are working in innovation, so they're actually more inclined to see themselves as creative than the average person!

If we don't believe we're creative, we can't consciously access our own creativity, and we're even less able to access group creativity. In the meantime, too many people shut down, because they're frustrated about trying to solve challenges without the awareness and understanding of the thinking processes involved in creativity or the ability to share their creative perspective and ideas.

Because this topic is almost never taught in schools, universities, or in the workplace, we're not fully aware of our own thinking process, or how other people's thinking processes differ from our own. Rarely do we have a shared knowledge of an efficient and clear group thinking process that can help us solve problems together.

■ The Core of Creativity

Too often when we talk about creativity, we discuss the virtue of frameworks or tools. I wanted to start at a broader level by introducing basic principles that underline creativity and innovation.

Three critical concepts

I learned three critical concepts about creativity on day one of graduate school.

First, we're *all* creative.

As human beings, we're solving problems that we haven't encountered before—all the time. To do that, we need to use creative thinking.

The standard definition of creativity is too narrowly focused on a certain outcome that tends to be related to the art world, so we think creativity is neither an important skill, nor one we all have or want to cultivate.

While studying creativity, I looked at many definitions of creativity and innovation. I've since narrowed this down to the ones I use most in my work:

> **Creativity is novelty that is useful.** This concept is widely used in the world of creativity and emphasizes that creativity needs to have a purpose, because something new without benefit to users is not really creative. One can argue that this includes art, as the purpose of art is to communicate feelings and issues in the world, as well as bringing joy, awe, and a different way of connecting to emotions. With this definition, creativity is in the hands of those who can appreciate it, and it's highly subjective.
>
> **Innovation is the ability to scale creativity.** This requires collaboration among teams. For me, innovation is about applying creativity effectively to create change.

Even if scholars agree on the novelty and usefulness elements, there are many discussions and much research about how to assess these objectively. As a practitioner, I believe the best way to evaluate creativity is by focusing on the outcomes, as defined by the team and/or management, as well as by those affected by these outcomes (whom we often call users).

There's no absolute and objective way to measure if an individual or a team is innovative, but success is relative to the goal and expected outcomes:

Was the problem clarified?

Did we get unstuck?

Did something new emerge that can be taken forward and implemented?

Did we meet our goals with a solution that fits our criteria?

No return after life? These could be functional, social, or emotional, and they could make their lives better, easier, cheaper, more meaningful, less stressful, etc.

Second, the real and meaningful question is, "In what ways are we creative?"

Once we establish that we're all creative as we continuously problem solve in our personal and professional lives, the next question is what type of thinking is more natural to us? What are our preferences?

That's where the concept of diversity of thinking and preferences is critical. Research from Reynolds and Lewis highlights that one obstacle to creating and embracing cognitive diversity is that "cognitive diversity is less visible."[9] For most of us, the way we think is unconscious. Too often, we assume that others think like us, using the same process. Or, if they don't, we think they should.

---

[9]Reynolds, A., & Lewis, D. (2017). Teams solve problems faster where they're more cognitively diverse. *Harvard Business Review*. https://hbr.org/2017/03/teams-solve-problems-faster-when-theyre-more-cognitively-diverse?autocomplete=true.

Third, creativity can be learned.

The Creative Studies Project, designed by Syd Parnes with Ruth Noller, studied the impact of four semesters of creativity training among students at SUNY Buffalo in the '70s. The results showed that creativity can be learned and that this impacts both overall college life and non-academic creative performance.[10, 11]

After this study, they began to consider how to teach creativity, both in classrooms (where programs are still too few and far apart) and in organizations. It's possible for all of us to leverage our own creativity by first becoming aware of the ways we're creative, then leveraging those skills—particularly if we learn how to do this effectively.

Why is it so important to understand how we think?
How does this boost our ability to think together creatively?

Consider the term **wicked problems**. This was first described by design theorists Rittel and Webber in 1973 and applied to planning.[12] Wicked problems are problems that can't be fully solved, because the solutions adopted will create other problems that would have been impossible to anticipate.[13] Think about issues like global warming or poverty or, even more timely, what's happening with AI. Every solution we adopt could have a positive impact, and yet it's likely to create new problems that we could not have anticipated.

Compare the world we are in now to the way things were before the COVID-19 pandemic. Who could have anticipated a worldwide epidemic, massive supply chain disruptions, or the need for remote work and study for months on end on a global basis? Whether you're an expert on these topics or just trying to buy enough supplies to get through the week, this affected you. The aspects of the pandemic cut across so many issues from medical and technology, to supply chain, social justice, politics, climate change, and others.

This crisis has also shown us that a team of experts isolated in a bubble can't solve complex issues. Medical experts had early insights about the virus, and scientists were able to come

---

[10]Parnes, S. J., & Noller, R. B. (1972). Applied creativity: The creative studies project, Part II. Results of the two-year program. *Journal of Creative Behavior*, 6(3), 164–186.

[11]Parnes, S. J., & Noller, R. B. (1973). Applied creativity: The creative studies project, Part IV. Personality findings and conclusions. *Journal of Creative Behavior*, 7(1), 15–36.

[12]Horst R., & W. J.; Webber, Melvin M. (1973). "*Dilemmas in a General Theory of Planning*" *(PDF). Policy Sciences. 4 (2): 155–169. doi:10.1007/bf01405730. S2CID 18634229.* Archived from the original (PDF) on 30 September 2007. [Reprinted in Cross, N., ed. (1984). v bggg. Chichester, England: John Wiley & Sons. pp. 135–144.]

[13] Camilius J.C (2008). Strategy as a Wicked Problem. *Harvard Business Review*. https://hbr.org/2008/05/strategy-as-a-wicked-problem.

up with a vaccine incredibly quickly,[14] but there were other technical challenges, including manufacturing and distributing vaccines, navigating the political issues at stake in each country, and understanding the global geopolitical implications of the pandemic. As a result, even now that the epidemic is officially over, there are still many incomplete and open issues likely to affect the next crisis, for instance the backlash about vaccines and mask use.

Early COVID-19 Testing: An example of epic failure

In the beginning of the epidemic, the US Center for Disease Control (CDC) was the sole supplier of tests to identify the presence of the COVID-19 virus. The problem was the initial tests sent out by the CDC had flaws, including primers that could bind to other primers and create false positives. Because of the way they were manufactured, the tests could also be contaminated with synthetic fragments of the virus. To compound the issue, the CDC did not cooperate with other clinical or commercial labs or allow the labs to distribute their own tests, therefore significantly delaying the US ability to test for COVID-19 altogether.[15] This is a perfect example of what happens when experts stay within their own narrow box, focus on power and politics, and don't communicate across teams and institutions, rather than having diverse minds and approaches focused on solving problems.

[14]It actually took only an hour to make the Moderna vaccine. Moore, M. (2022). *How mrna medicine will change the world* [Video]. TED. https://www.ted.com/talks/melissa_j_moore_how_mrna_medicine_will_change_the_world?language=en.
[15]C.D.C. Virus tests were contaminated and poorly designed agency said. Anthes, E. (2021). *New York Times*, December 15, 2021 https://www.nytimes.com/2021/12/15/health/cdc-covid-tests-contaminated.html?searchResultPosition=2.

It's likely that your team members already think diversely.

Highly successful organizations work to maximize that. But there's an opportunity to make that diversity of thinking more explicit, as it will impact the outcome and the work of the team.

A 2017 Reynolds and Lewis study shows that groups with cognitive diversity (differences in perspective or information processing style) perform significantly better than homogeneous teams.[16] An internal innovation study done by IBM showed that teams who are consciously aware of how they think (both individually and as a team), as well as the processes they use to solve problem collaboratively, are more likely to be successful.[17]

Now it's your turn to experiment and reflect on your way of thinking. Set aside time to write down your answers and to reflect on what you've written.

Because you were under a time constraint (unless you ignored the instructions all together, which is also related to a thinking preference), you likely used your default or preferred mode of thinking, which it turned out is likely to be different from that of others. Yet, often we aren't aware that the way we solve problems is different. That's why we need to understand different ways of thinking, which we'll go into more detail in the following chapters.

Once team members understand this, they say, "Aha—now I get it. This is why you do things that way. Now I see you and you see me. We can collaborate. The person with the best skill for each part of the problem can work on that part. We can make great things happen together."

[16]Reynolds, A. & Lewis, D. (2017). 17 DeCusatis, C. (2008).
[17]DeCusatis, C. (2008). Creating, Growing and Sustaining Efficient Innovation Teams. *Creativity and Innovation Management,* 17(2), 155–164.

Practice #1:
Solve a Challenge Quickly

Use this QR code to download a journal with all the practices in the book so you can write in your answers.

Decide where to take your next vacation and how to prepare for the trip.

Take five minutes to write down everything that comes to mind related to this trip and come up with a plan.

....

....

Reflect on your thinking process. What did you do during these five minutes, and how did you come to a solution? This is likely to be the default mode you use to solve problems.

....

....

Then ask one or two other friends, co-workers, or family members to do the same. When they're done, discuss and compare notes on how this worked. How are their processes different? How are they similar?

....

....

How were the outcomes different or similar? Why do you think it was similar or different?

....

....

Reflect and write down what you learned from this experience. Note at least three things you discovered through this observation.

....

....

Chapter 2

Igniting the Innovation Engine: *Understanding the Innovation Process*

A few years ago, I got a call from one of the founders of a small fashion company. Ruth and her co-founder Angela had a challenging time moving their business forward and requested my help.

I soon realized that their team was good at creating ideas for products—very good at this, in fact. Their problem wasn't that they didn't have *enough* ideas, but that they had *too many* and didn't know what to do with them. The team knew how to work with the supply chain, get samples, and create great collections that were loved by their customers. The back end of the business was easy: It was the front end that was hard. They didn't have a clear way to identify opportunities for growth, or to sort through new ideas for their collections. They asked me to help put a process in place that could be shared with all team members to develop a common framework and tools that they could use on their own.

First, we used the **FourSight® Thinking Profile** tool[18] (which we will discuss in more detail in Chapter 3) to understand each team member's preferences for different parts of the process, and to see how the team dynamics worked. We realized that differences in the ways team members were thinking were obstacles to the smooth functioning of the organization—particularly given the profile of the co-founders, each of whom had a very different preference.

Then, I worked with the team to put in place basic training using an approach called **design thinking**, a methodology that was initially started in the 70s and made more popular by the consulting firm IDEO 30 years ago (see details on page 85).[19] We outlined the key steps in the process and the tools they needed to be effective. I created a two-day workshop that started by identifying the problems they were trying to solve with the business, then addressed how to create and evaluate ideas and develop them into prototypes. We then brought users into the process, and developed a way to test, evaluate, and iterate on ideas quickly. This allowed the team to narrow the choices down to a few concepts that would go to designers and suppliers moving forward. They still came up with just as many, if not more, ideas, but now they had a clear process on what to do with them.

At times, it was challenging for them to appreciate what each person brought to the effort. The process was often cut short when one founder had an idea. The team rushed off to execute, which resulted in many failures. They didn't leave enough time to get through the process properly, particularly the development/prototyping and testing stage. Identifying their innovation profiles helped the founders and the team understand how to work with the rest of the team more effectively. Creating a common process, language, and tools helped the team be sure they would not skip steps, and allowed them to work together in a constructive and systematic way—regardless of which steps needed to happen and each person's thinking preference. As a result, they were able to save time and bring designs to market faster.

> Creating a common process, language, and tools helped the team be sure they would not skip steps, and allowed them to work together in a constructive and systematic way—regardless of which steps needed to happen and each person's thinking preference.

---

[18]https://www.foursightonline.com/team-assessment.
[19]https://www.interaction-design.org/literature/article/design-thinking-get-a-quick-overview-of-the-history.

■ A Quick Background about Creativity and Innovation

Space doesn't allow me to list all the names of the giants who frame our current thinking on creativity, but I want to provide a short introduction to the origin of the creativity movement.

Alex Osborn was one of the founders of the iconic advertising agency BBDO (he was the O). In the 1940s and '50s, Osborn wanted to find a way to make his teams more creative so they could generate more ideas. He started formalizing ways of thinking that could help team creativity. While he invented the word and concept of brainstorming (for which he is remembered) in his 1963 book *Applied Imagination: Principles and Procedures of Creative Thinking*, Osborn did much more than create a tool. He designed a whole process called **Creative Problem Solving** that outlined each step from identifying the problem to getting to an implementable solution.

> *"Creativity is an art, an applied art, a workable art, a teachable art, a learnable art, an art in which all of us can make ourselves more and more proficient."*
>
> Alex Osborn, Applied Imagination,[20] 1963

Many of these fundamentals, including elements of the framework, principles, and tools, have since been adapted to other creative processes, such as design thinking, lean thinking, and agile management—often without an awareness of the historic connections.

---

[20]Osborn, A. F. (1963). *Applied imagination: Principles and procedures of creative problem-solving (3rd Rev. ed.)*. Charles Scribner's Sons.

The Universal Approach to Solving Problems

While there are many different models for innovation and problem solving, with different numbers of steps at the core, there's a somewhat universal process that needs to happen to solve problems, change, and innovate.

This is summarized in the FourSight® Innovation Process:

- **Clarify the situation** to understand the challenge and ensure you are working on the most meaningful/important/relevant issue.
- **Generate ideas** to solve the challenge.
- **Develop solutions** by finding ways to make the ideas feasible.
- **Implement plans** and take action to make the solutions happen.

Clarify   **Ideate**   **Develop**   **Implement**

Source: FourSight® model: Nielsen, D., Thurber, S., based on Puccio, G. J. Miller, B. J., 2003.

For example, if your problem is around hosting the next Thanksgiving dinner, you could think about the following:

What is the situation? We have in town and out-of-town guests. One niece is vegan. Uncle Joe often drinks too much and may tell offensive jokes. Grandma doesn't want to host this year. Aunt Jill wants to bring her caramelized yams that are never eaten. *You have to decide what the challenge is. For example, the challenge could be how to have a dinner with vegan options at a new host place. Or, how to have a dinner without family drama. Or, how to simplify the Thanksgiving dinner process.*

Ideation. Let's say you decide to solve the first challenge. You may then come up with 50 ideas and decide which are the top ten you will consider. Host at a restaurant. Have a progressive dinner, so nobody has to host the whole day. Ask Aunt Jill to make her yams recipe vegan. Only have a couple of bottles of wine. Ask Aunt Jill to host, but let her know she doesn't have to cook, as everyone will bring a vegan and a non-vegan dish. Talk to Uncle Joe ahead of time about his jokes.

Develop solutions. You want to explore the restaurant options, so you check a few that offer a Thanksgiving menu with vegan option. You try two restaurants to see if you like them. You get feedback from family members that they don't want to be eating out at a restaurant for a family meal. Ask Aunt Jill to make a version of her yam recipe vegan (surprisingly, it's quite good!). Talk to Uncle Joe and explain how his jokes make the younger generation uncomfortable. Get Aunt Annie and her son John, who live close to each other, to host the main meal, respectively, and then move for desserts, as long as they don't have to cook it all.

Implement. Assign each family a dish to cook and bring to Aunt Annie's (including three vegan options). Make sure Aunt Jill brings her now vegan yams. Have dessert served at John's, with only a few bottles of champagne (which limits Uncle Joe's after-meal drinking). As a result, Grandma tells you she enjoyed Thanksgiving again, since she doesn't have to do so much preparation, cooking, and cleaning at her place. And Uncle Joe only told one bad joke!

This may seem like a lot of work but consider the outcome for the family to get a much less stressful and enjoyable holiday!

This is an example of a personal situation, but this way of thinking can be used to make all kinds of outcomes much better and more efficient!

■ Innovation Takes Many Forms

We can classify innovation by the area involved (for example, product, service, business model, technology, process, social, or environmental) and by the degree of innovation (from small, incremental innovation to major, transformative innovation).

> **Most innovations are incremental, and they may be important or critical just to keep up with our times.**

Incremental innovation, which involves tweaking a feature here and there, is often not considered to be "real" innovation. Sometimes, it includes modifications that are of interest to few people or with small impact. Think about a new flavor of M&Ms, or yet another update to your cell phone. But the reality is that most innovations are incremental, and they may be important or critical just to keep up with our times. For example, innovation in processes that can save money or time (such as automating steps or making the process more environmentally friendly), or finding a different angle to approach a standard business (like a food delivery company that offers imperfect foods and surplus)[21] can be meaningful and necessary in their own ways.

Major innovation includes large changes which fundamentally modify the way we behave, interact, and think. Often, this requires changing core assumptions of how things actually exist and finding new ways to look at a business—such as changing assumptions around existing business models.

Think about the changes over the last few decades in how music is distributed: from vinyl to CDs to the immediate purchase of albums on your phone to infinite access on the cloud with Spotify or other platforms, without the need to own any music anymore.

Similarly, travel accommodation transformed from hotels owned by companies and individual homes rented through agencies to include new options from shared ownership through time share or fractional ownership to peer-to-peer rentals of personal homes via VRBO and Airbnb.

---

[21]Imperfect Foods. *Home page*. Imperfect Foods https://www.imperfectfoods.com.

Of course, the latest and likely extremely disruptive innovation, both in scale and pace, is AI. While artificial intelligence has been around in many forms for years, the recent release of ChatGPT to all was quickly followed by AI tools from Microsoft, Google, and many other companies. The resulting FOMO (fear of missing out) led to a frenzied attempt to integrate AI into all kinds of businesses. As of summer 2023, when this book was written, it's unclear what the full global impact of AI will be. I would argue though, that understanding the principles and process of innovation is even more critical, given the accelerated pace of change.

Innovation can also be classified by the type of problems (known or unknown) and by whether it's closed or open. In **closed innovation**, organizations look internally to find solutions. With **open innovation**, external partners are also involved, either in a public way (such as projects financed by the XPRIZE foundation)[22] or with external partners tied to a specific challenge (such as customers, research institutions, or suppliers).

Innovation is critical to the survival of most organizations. If you don't change in a world where everything else changes around you—including your customer's needs and wants, your competition, technologies, expectations, and norms—then you'll become obsolete. Remember Blockbuster and ToysRus? These are two organizations that failed to adapt. Interestingly, ToysRus is trying to reinvent themselves after going out of business in 2018 by starting a partnership with Macy's to sell toys online under the Macy's brand and create stores within Macy's stores for the 2022 holiday season.[23] On the other hand, Netflix was able to pivot from mailing CDs to digital distribution of movies and TV shows, and, finally, to producing their own content and distributing it worldwide.

> **Innovation is critical to the survival of most organizations. If you don't change in a world where everything else changes around you—including your customer's needs and wants, your competition, technologies, expectations, and norms—then you'll become obsolete.**

---

[22]XPRIZE (n.d). *Home page*. XPRIZE www.xprize.org.
[23]NPR (2022, July 19). *Toys R Us is making another come back—this time in Macy's stores*. NPR. https://www.npr.org/2022/07/19/1112275498/toys-r-us-macys-stores.

I've found that in organizations—particularly large corporations—there is a bias towards not changing, because change means taking risks, possibly disrupting well-managed systems and needing to convince too many people. Too often, though, the risk of *not* changing is not well-evaluated. Researchers Daniel Kahneman and Amos Tversky have described our risk-adverse biases. Their **prospect theory** explains that even if potential winnings are higher than losses, most of us prefer not to take the risk. We wildly overvalue what we have, and we undervalue opportunity. This risk-aversion has negative consequences, both in our daily lives and in organizations.[24]

This is how I like to illustrate this concept.

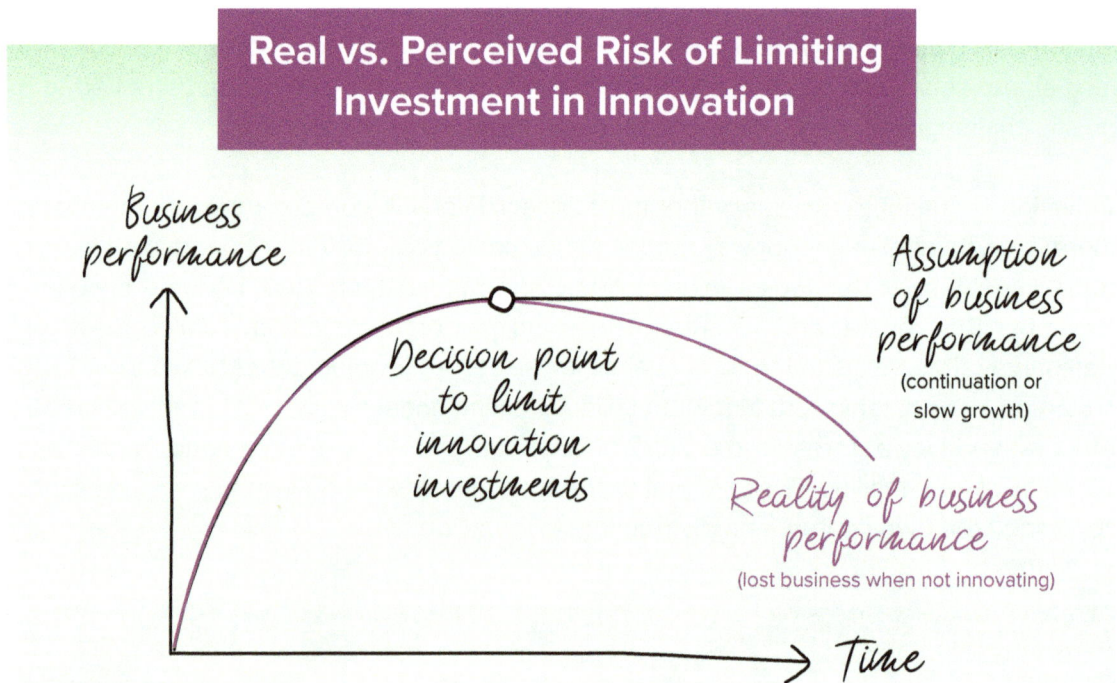

Real vs. Perceived Risk of Limiting Investment in Innovation

Business performance

Decision point to limit innovation investments

Assumption of business performance
(continuation or slow growth)

Reality of business performance
(lost business when not innovating)

Time

Even sectors that seem really generic have learned to innovate over time. Think about how the chocolate market evolved in the past 30 years—from basic Hershey bars and M&Ms to thousands of variations based on bean origins, diets, new flavors, consistency, and sustainable farming practices.

[24]Kahneman, D., & Tversky, A. (1979). Prospect theory: an analysis of decisions under risk. *Econometrica*, 47(2), 263–291.

■ Thinking Practically about Innovation

Start with the users.

When you think about innovation, it's important to first understand your users (meaning all those who may be affected by your proposed changes), their challenges (what's working, what's not working for them, what could be improved, and why it's important to do so), and your domain (not from a silo mentality but from the perspective of the human needs) to make changes that address the right problems in a meaningful way.

For example, when I was working for a startup focused on interior design, we went to peoples' homes to understand how they approach designing their homes and picking up furniture and accessories. We also talked to designers, as well as, to people selling furniture. From this work, we learned that the challenges for the people decorating their home was the overwhelming choices of options that often left them unable to make a purchase. For many, hiring a personal interior designer was not seen as an option for cost reasons as well as often thinking it was not worth it for only a piece of furniture or two. From this work with the users came the idea of offering online interior design help at a very affordable cost.

Whether you use the design thinking process that puts users at the core of the process (see page 85) or another approach, there will be an impact (good, bad, or sometimes both) on people who will need to do things differently or handle different outcomes, so it's best to consider them front and center in your innovation work

Innovation requires us to let go of assumptions.

Assumptions allow us to go faster and to build on our previous experiences. While they may help save time and be efficient, assumptions are often a disservice in innovation if we don't make a conscious effort to make them transparent and aren't willing to challenge them.

For example, the COVID-19 pandemic forced us to give up many assumptions quickly. Many companies had strongly affirmed that working from home wasn't possible, but when the pandemic hit, that assumption was blown away.

> **Assumptions are often a disservice in innovation if we don't make a conscious effort to make them transparent and aren't willing to challenge them.**

It turned out it actually was possible to have remote knowledge worker employees living in different locations. Since then, some highly effective virtual teams have never even met in person. Many organizations are now considering or have implemented a hybrid model, allowing a part of their workforce to work fully or partially remotely.

Think about all the disruptions in the supply chain during the pandemic. Organizations had focused on the least expensive way to make products, assuming it would always be possible to ship goods across the world. I was amused by the story about the lack of toilet paper on shelves at the beginning of the pandemic. While the rumor was that it was caused by people hoarding toilet paper, the reality is there was a change in behavior. People were using more toilet paper at home, since they were now working remotely, and toilet paper was no longer used in bulk in many office buildings. It turns out there are two separate channels of paper product distribution with different packaging and sizes, so while toilet paper was sparse in the supermarkets, there was an excess in the commercial circuit.

Reflection

What do you think were the assumptions in the toilet paper shortage?

How might challenging them upfront have avoided this crisis?

Good innovation processes are broad.

Many innovation approaches overfocus on specific tools. They start with ideas or hypotheses and go directly to commercialization, missing a few steps along the way.

With AI, it's easy to be excited by the tools and lose sight of the big picture. In five minutes, AI could give you a business idea (or 100), or even a business plan and logo. It could test this with virtual users, but that's not likely to guarantee success (and remember that tool may be offering the exact same idea to everyone else too.

Here are the criteria for a good innovation process:

- Start by **understanding the environment** and the challenges at hand. Don't assume you already know the answer.
- **Consider ideation** as a small and not-so-important part of the process. This may sound surprising, but my experience working with groups is that if you have a good facilitator and process, coming up with ideas is the easier part of the process (and with AI even easier.) The before (defining the right problem) and after (developing and implementing the ideas) are more challenging.
- **Be iterative**, since innovation is not a linear process.
- **Integrate users** throughout.
- **Be flexible**, since ultimately you can't fully predict how the journey will progress. The challenge itself may evolve and the solutions may not work, forcing you to back track.

The innovation process is iterative, messy, and not linear.

Innovation is, first and foremost, a learning journey. There's no way to predict what you may learn while moving through the process, and what you learn informs what you need to do next. Thinking about innovation as nonlinear helps adopt a mindset of being open to whatever may happen. It's unlikely that any innovation process will take a team from the beginning to the end in a neat, linear way. Organizations often fight this with tight deadlines and an expectation that things will keep moving straight forward—no matter what. Most likely, they'll see forward motion, but not without some back-and-forth and unexpected detours in the journey. Sometimes you will even need to go back to the drawing board and start over again. The nature of innovation is to work with the unknown in a world of ambiguity, where things happen in an unpredictable way, in an environment that also keeps changing. You may have heard the term VUCA. Originally created in the army, this is an acronym for Volatile, Uncertain, Complex, and Ambiguous, and it's a good description of the context around innovation work.[25]

Innovation is messy and non linear

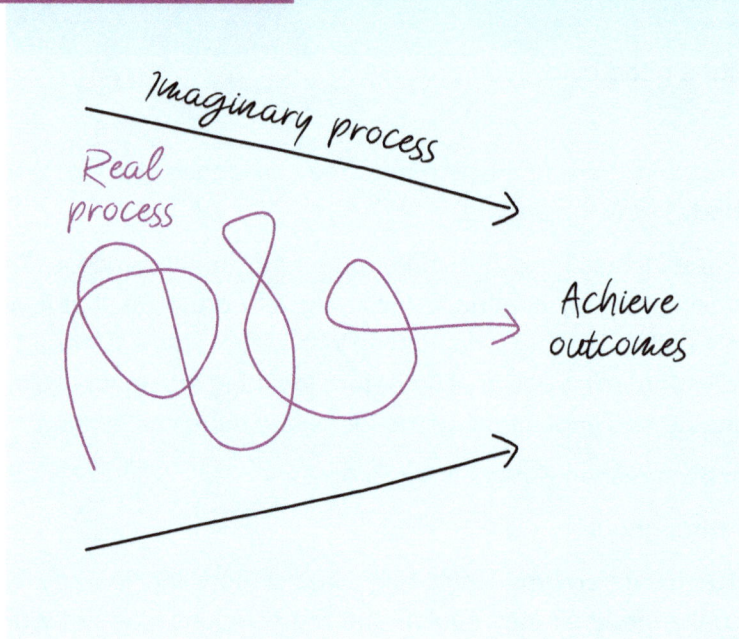

Imaginary process

Real process

Achieve outcomes

Failure is part of the process.

Failure is, by nature, a part of the innovation process. It's important to understand what failure is and what it's not, and to know the type of failure you actually want to embrace in a successful innovation process.

When we use the word failure, it's easy to think of epic failure—those mistakes that kill businesses. This is when something terrible happens and you want to hide, cover up, or move on quickly.

---

[25]Peschi, M., & Mation, M. (2021, February). What is the meaning of a Vuca world? *The Living Core.* https://www.thelivingcore.com/en/what-is-the-meaning-of-vuca-world/.

A classic example is how simple O-rings destroyed a space shuttle. The Challenger explosion in 1986 was caused by the failure of O-rings that ensured the integrity of the shuttle during take-off. These inexpensive parts were impacted by cold weather. There were many warnings about the issues, both from NASA and from the engineers at Morton Thiokol, who designed the part. However, management chose to ignore or deny the existence of the problem, rather than ensuring it would be solved. Because such issues were considered bad failures, they were ignored. In this case, the failure had terrible consequences![26]

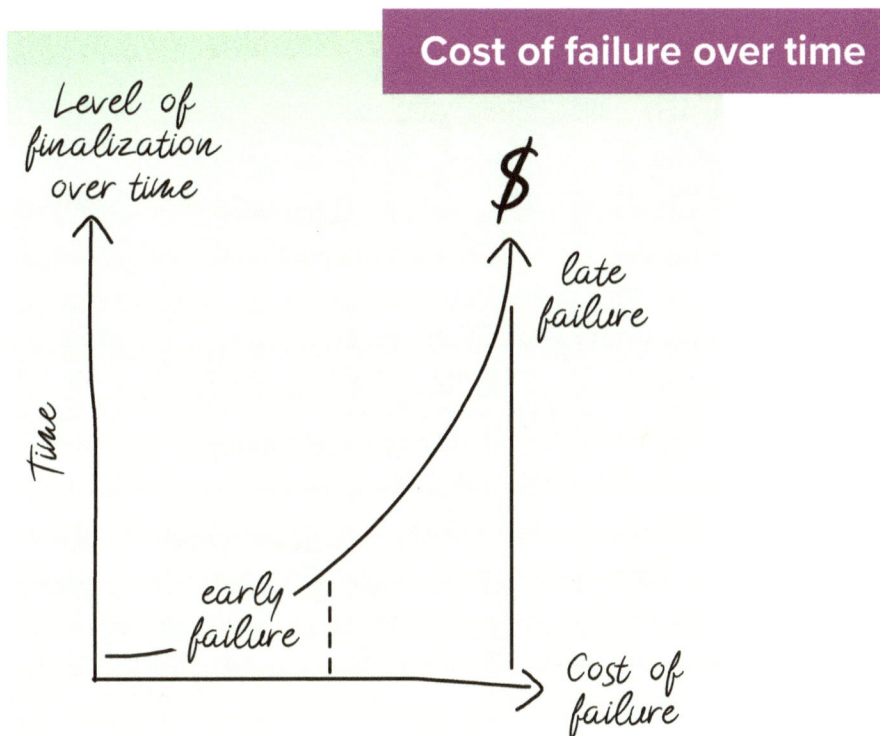

Cost of failure over time

Consider that 75% of startups and more than 90% of new products fail—and those are major failures. Large companies and organizations fail and go out of business. If you look at the failures of large organizations over the past 20 years, it's actually more likely that the lack of innovation and the inability to adapt to a changing environment ultimately killed these businesses, rather than too much failed innovation. For example, some major companies totally missed the trend of online selling (Borders bookstore), or the move to digital (Kodak and Blockbuster, again), or they stopped innovating altogether (GM went bankrupt, but was reborn after a government bailout as a very innovative company).

---

[26]*Investigation of the Challenger Accident*, (House Report 99-1016). House of Representatives ninety-ninth congress. https://www.govinfo.gov/content/pkg/GPO-CRPT-99hrpt1016/pdf/GPO-CRPT-99hrpt1016.pdf.

Then there are small failures—planned failures that help you learn on your journey—or even bigger failures that could be interpreted as opportunities to learn and transform in the future. Innovation projects should build in failure as part of learning, but also find ways to limit the impact in what we call **managed failure**, or **controlled failure**. This means minimizing the impact by failing early and often, when it's less expensive and has less impact on the organization and the outcomes.

What does it take to embrace failure?

An innovative organization allows failure and makes it safe to fail. A. G. Lafley, former CEO of Procter & Gamble, said, "We learn much more from failure than we do from success."[27] But this is only if the organization is willing to accept the consequences of failure!

> *"We learn much more from failure than we do from success."*
>
> – A. G. Lafley, former CEO of Procter & Gamble

If you try something new—an idea, suggestion, concept, way to partner, way to work, or even changing the people on your team—it may not work perfectly, or it might even fail totally. If you're then put on the sideline, made wrong for trying or, worse yet, demoted or fired, then you'll no longer risk trying to innovate in the future.

It takes a lot to create an innovative environment, but not much to shut it down.

The mottos, slogans, or messages that an organization uses to encourage innovation don't really matter. If the behaviors of managers and peers are not aligned, this will be seen as lip service, and it will kill innovation in its tracks. This is one of the reasons large corporations often innovate by purchasing startups or creating separate startup-like units. They know that the existing culture will likely kill new ideas before they have a chance to gestate. Too often, when a company purchases a startup for its innovative ideas and then integrates it into their existing business system, innovation dies as a result. For example, Starbucks bought a chain of bakery called La Boulange for $100 million and closed all the stores two years later.[28]

---

[27]Lafley, A. G., & Charan, R. (2008). *The Game-Changer: How you can drive revenue and profit growth with innovation.* Crown Business Group.
[28]https://www.fool.com/investing/2017/05/22/i-still-cant-believe-starbucks-corporation-spent-1.aspx.

Taking a Different View

Instead of being scared of failure, we need to plan for and organize failure as powerful lessons to learn and ways to improve. In innovation, the best way to fail is to test as early and as cheaply as possible. If failure is built into testing (which should be started as soon as possible) and seen as a learning experience, then it becomes part of the process. When ideas are tried and tested with customers, it's likely that many of them won't be well-received or understood. But having that information early in the process will provide great data to iterate, improve, retest, and move on.

Too often, organizations develop a culture of perfection. Employees and managers want to have all the charts in a row. They want all the information before any of it is shared to ensure they won't fail. **A culture of perfection hurts innovation**. Instead, you may want to share as much

> **Rather than wondering whether we can afford to fail, we should consider if we can afford *not* to fail. It's better to anticipate and manage failure upfront then to be surprised when failure occurs.**

as possible very early in the process—even if it's rough and work in progress. This could be an understanding of the problem, a hypothesis, possible ideas, ways to implement a solution, etc.

How can you encourage your team to create prototypes and test early? When I pose this question to the teams with whom I've worked, they're often puzzled, as they think their idea lacks enough pieces to be tested. Or, because it's not a physical product, it can't be tested. Once you challenge these assumptions, there are always ways to create a prototype and get feedback.

I worked with a startup creating a new platform for offering online interior design services. We spent the first year learning and testing our ideas without any engineering involvement. PowerPoint presentations and image boards were a substitute for our concepts, and yet we learned a lot and were able to iterate and improve at minimal cost. Boards, flow charts, skits, short videos, and wireframes are all great ways to prototype during early stages when failure will likely be quick and cheap. Only once you learn as much as you can should you consider scaling up progressively, as each iteration is likely to represent more time, more people involved, and more money invested.

Rather than wondering whether we can afford to fail, we should consider if we can afford *not* to fail. It's better to anticipate and manage failure upfront then to be surprised when failure occurs. By not failing early, you're more likely eventually to fail big-time, as business as usual may not be sustainable while the environment around you is in flux.

When we fail, it's important to focus on the learning—understanding what went wrong, what to change or fix, and how to do better next time—rather than pointing fingers. Postmortem debriefs are really important, as you can't move on and hope not to reproduce the same problems if you don't spend time consciously understanding what actually caused the failure.

One of my grad school professors gave each of us a quota of ten errors. We asked what would happen when we used our quota. She told us we would get another set of ten! The same thing happens in improv classes where failure is embraced. Failing, being silly, having the scene not working well, and not following the rules of a game all become a shared and delightful exercise.

Knowing that failure is likely to be part of your innovation process, embracing it, including it (particularly early and cheaply), and celebrating it will likely help you avoid the big failures—including the one that may be too costly to survive.

Embracing success too!

When a team is successful, we often acknowledge and sometimes celebrate the outcome, but less frequently do we look at the process and the positive lessons learned. This means we miss an opportunity to bring to light and then reuse the unique lessons of a successful project and a successful team that could then be leveraged across the organization. Stan Hou, an executive with whom I worked, summarized it nicely. "I've often found that learning from *success* doesn't get done enough. Experimentation can result in both success and failure, and I think it's just as important to understand why something succeeded (as opposed to what most teams do of going, 'Phew. That worked. Let's move on to the next thing.')."

Practice #2:
Embracing Failure

Think about a time you failed. This could be in your personal life, work life, or anywhere, and it should not be a major failure, but more of an everyday failure.

When ....

....

I felt that I/we failed because ....

....

The results of this failure were ....

....

I did / did not *(circle which one applies)* reflect on this failure because

....

Now that I can look at this from a distance, I realize there were lessons learned:

#1: ....

#2: ....

#3: ....

If I had embraced that failure differently, I could have ....

....

In the future, I want to deal with failure by ....

....

Chapter 3

Diversity: *The Fuel for Powerful Innovation*

I was helping a team create the invitation for a five-hour virtual event. Being new to this group, I asked if we were expecting people to stay for the entire event. If so, how might we communicate about this upfront, so that we didn't have people coming in and out, thinking that it didn't matter and not realizing the impact on the team and the outcome.

No one had thought about this question during their previous events. My comment triggered a long discussion about clarifying purpose and our ask from attendees, so they would have the best experience. We ended up inviting attendees to consider the full five-hour time frame as an opportunity to create space for themselves and to be fully engaged in the discussions. We pointed out how important it was for them to stay through the entire event.

Why was this important? Without my way of thinking (which naturally goes to clarifying issues), the invitation may not have mentioned the time commitment. It's likely that we may have had some attendees attending late and others leaving early—which would have greatly affected the ability to create deep discussions and connections among the full group.

When we create together, bringing diversity of thinking, as well as other forms of diversity, can make a significant difference in the outcome.

There are many forms of diversity and they're all important and complementary

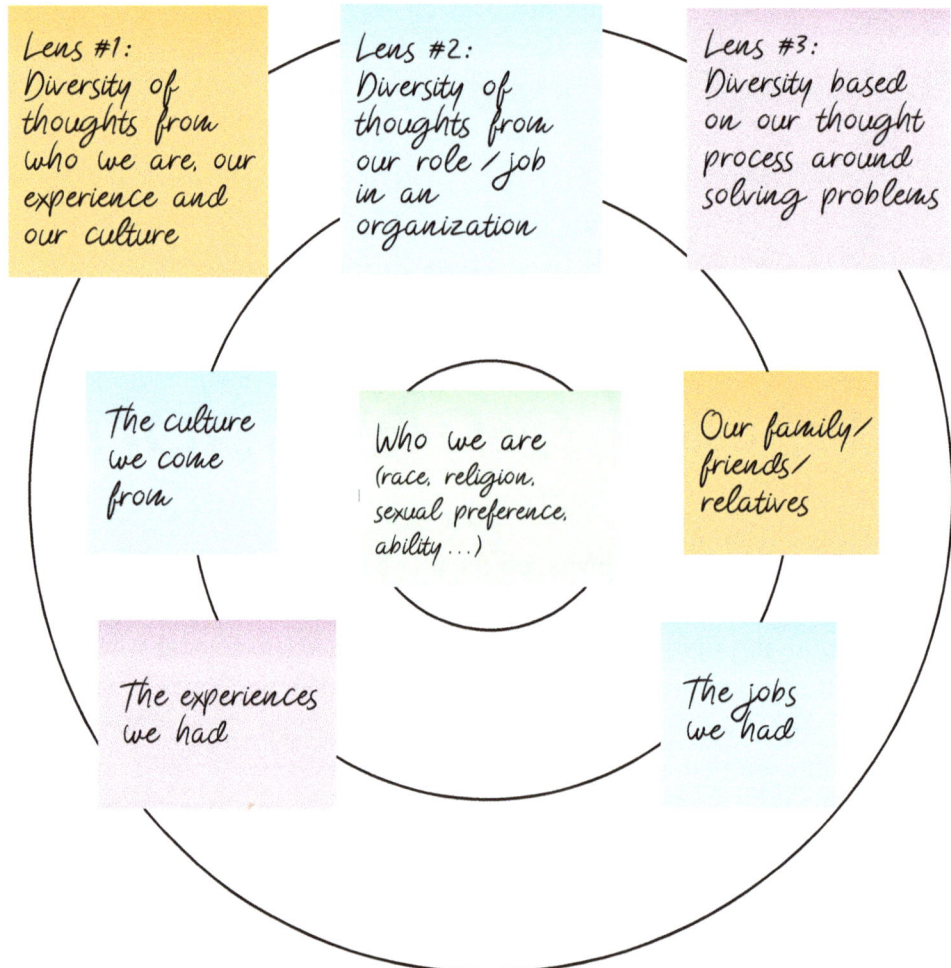

Lens #1:
Diversity of thoughts from who we are, our experience and our culture

Lens #2:
Diversity of thoughts from our role / job in an organization

Lens #3:
Diversity based on our thought process around solving problems

The culture we come from

Who we are (race, religion, sexual preference, ability ...)

Our family/ friends/ relatives

The experiences we had

The jobs we had

Elements that are important in defining diversity, beyond such inherent diversity elements as gender, race, age/generation, and sexual preference may include:

Who you are.
Your family of origin, your culture (in your family, your city, your country, your side of the world, your religion, your education, etc.).

Your history.
Schools attended, hobbies, physical, artistic, and spiritual practices.

Your values.
What is important for you—your work ethic, your professional and personal priorities, the type of environment in which you want to be.

Your personal and professional experience.
Jobs, functions, and organizations.

Other experiences that shape you and your way of thinking.

How we consider the challenge and how we solve it.

■ Why Diversity Is So Critical to Innovation

Teams dedicated to innovation or creating significant change face complex problems that require multiple perspectives. The most successful teams ensure they understand and solve the problems by including team members that each bring something unique—be it their identities, background, experiences, role in the organization, and also different ways of thinking. They aim to create solutions that will be appropriate for diverse users.

What happens when you don't do this? You may end up creating solutions that only work for people "like you" and exclude many others. In the tech world, particularly in engineering, there are still few women and people of color at the entry level—and even fewer in management positions. Very often, these individuals leave at a much higher pace than their male and white colleagues, because they find the culture toxic.[29] There's no guarantee that

---

[29]Catalyst (2022, August 23). Women in Science, Technology, Mathematics and Engineering (STEM) (Quick Take). Catalyst.org.

AI will be any better than human input, given that the LLMs (Learning Language Models) currently used by tools like ChatGPT are a black box—even for the companies that created them. It's unclear how the tool is learning or what biases are part of the programming. And the tools are trained using the internet, which as we know has biases built into the content.

Technology and diversity are strongly connected. Lenovo created a Product Diversity Office in 2020 focused on designing with diversity of users in mind. Their goal is to vet most of their products moving forward, particularly those that have the most likelihood of biases related to ableism and physical dimensions (such as hand shape, skin color, gender).[30]

When you create a future with new technologies and ideas created and developed with a non-diverse, homogeneous group, you're likely to leave a lot of people behind who will not benefit to the same extent (if at all) from the innovation. The health care area provides an important example.

Historically, research has been focused mostly on young (white) men, without considering the unique needs of women, older people, or those of different origins.[31]

Yet, despite the fact that there's no scientific basis to prove relevancy, race medicine, that is believing that interpretation of test results and symptoms should differ based on race (for example, the myth that people of color are not as sensitive to pain), is still widely used in this country to offer different levels of care based on race.[32]

■ Blowing Up Silo Thinking

Good solutions have multiple dimensions. Looking at them through only one lens is likely to miss problems and possibly lead to failures later on.

I had a client whose marketing group came up with a new product, tested it, and got very positive feedback from their customers. It took the company a year and a half to get to the stage where they decided they should talk to their manufacturing group. It turns out that this "perfect" idea had a multimillion-dollar negative impact on manufacturing, because it

[30]Wral News (2022, October 28). Lenovo incorporates diversity into product development. Wral.com https://www.wral.com/lenovo-incorporates-diversity-into-product-development/20541864/.

[31]Johnson, P. (2013). His and hers . . . heath care [Video]. TED. https://www.ted.com/talks/paula_johnson_his_and_hers_health_care?referrer=playlist-10_talks_by_women_that_everyon&autoplay=true.

[32]Roberts, D. (2015). *The problem with race-based medicine* [Video]. TED.https://www.ted.com/talks/dorothy_roberts_the_problem_with_race_based_medicine?language=en; and Olayiwola N. (2020). Combating racism and place-ism in medicine [Video]. TED https://www.ted.com/talks/j_nwando_olayiwola_combating_racism_and_place_ism_in_medicine.

would have required retooling and changing production lines. Once the cost was integrated, they realized the original idea was not financially sustainable. But the marketing group hadn't seen this, because they looked at the challenge from only one perspective, which didn't consider all aspects of the solution. This is what can happen with siloed thinking.

Large organizations tend to work in silos. People tend to work with people like them—this could be people in the same function or the same department, as well as people who come from similar demographic groups. Often, they also prefer to work with people who think like them. Managers also tend to hire people who think the way they do. They usually aren't aware of this bias—they simply find it easier to relate to people who think similarly.

> **When we work to solve complex problems, we can't work only with people "like us." We need to break the silos by valuing and cultivating diversity in perspectives and in thinking.**

As a young manager, I realized the pace of thinking for some people on my team was significantly different than mine. I tend to have many ideas, and I can think really quickly. Some of the people on my team needed more time to come up with ideas and solutions. This had nothing to do with the quality of the ideas they brought—it was just the way they processed information. At first, I was annoyed and frustrated that they wouldn't come up with answers right away, but with awareness I learned to appreciate their thoroughness. I realized I had to give them time and space to think, rather than requiring an immediate answer. And that positively transformed our ability to collaborate.

When we work to solve complex problems, we can't work only with people "like us." We need to break the silos by valuing and cultivating diversity in perspectives and in thinking.

If you want to create innovation that's meaningful and desirable to your end users, feasible for your organization, and financially profitable (or sustainable for nonprofits), you may want to bring different voices to your innovation teams early in the process.

Siloed Innovation

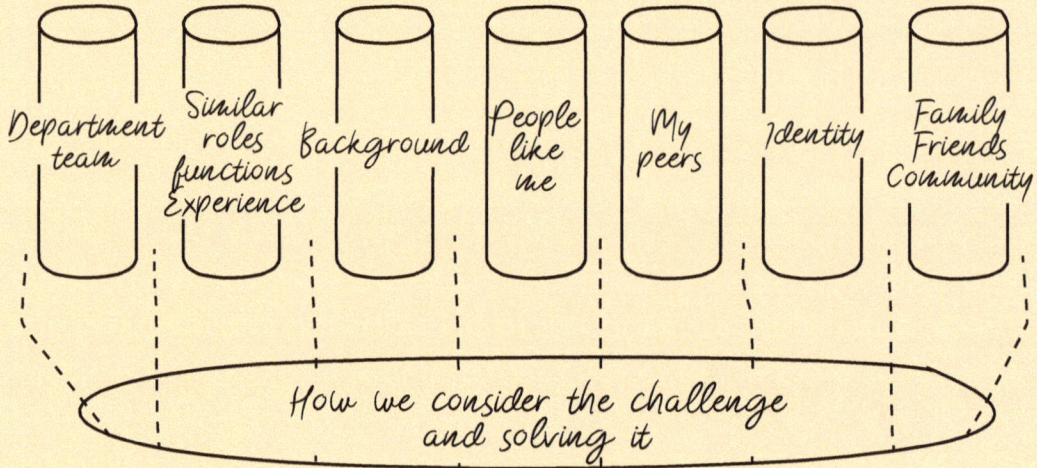

Department team | Similar roles functions Experience | Background | People like me | My peers | Identity | Family Friends Community

How we consider the challenge and solving it

Multi Perspective Innovation

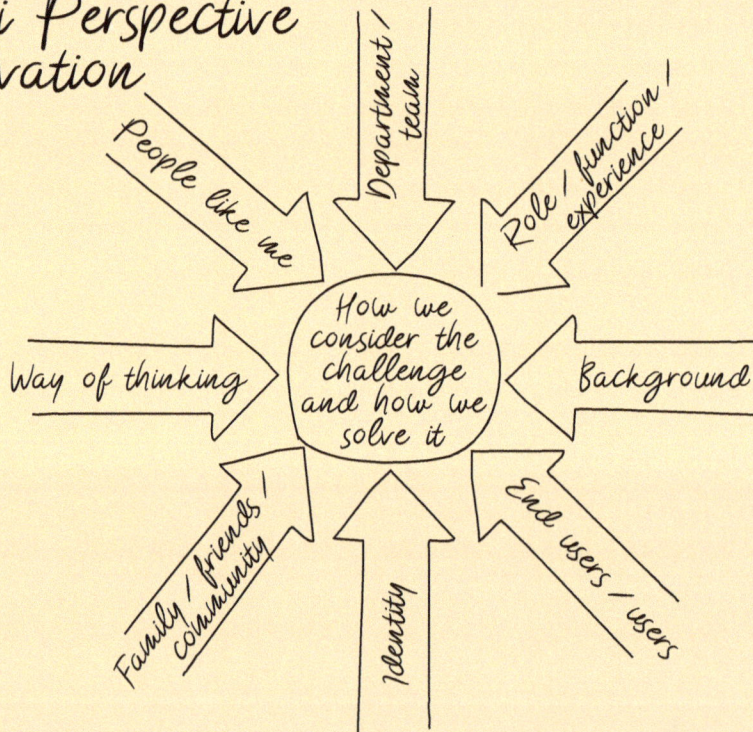

People like me

Department / team

Role / function / experience

Way of thinking

How we consider the challenge and how we solve it

Background

Family / friends / community

Identity

End users / users

The Elephant in the Room

When members of the team understand what's happening in team meetings—how and why each person interacts and behaves—it's a real eye opener. Team members are actually speaking different languages, but they don't know it.

Consider the Indian parable of a group of blind people who meet an elephant. Each person "sees" a certain piece—one feels the trunk; another, the tail; a third, the legs. But no one captures the whole animal. Each one makes assumptions of what an elephant may be: Is it hard and smooth? Wrinkled and hard? Straight and long?

The answer depends on what you touch. If I were working with this group, every member would come up with a different reality about what an elephant is. That could be an asset or a liability, depending on how you would handle these differences in perception.

Unconscious biases are like a blindfold that stops us from seeing the bigger picture. We don't appreciate what we can't see. With a team, we're usually not aware of the differences between how we think and how others do so. We have assumptions and assume they are truths; we build routines and expect people to follow them because that is "the right way."

■ Making Diverse Thinking Visible

Remember the different thinking activities required to solve problems and innovate that we discussed in the last chapter? Turns out that we each have preferences for different parts of that process. When we're engaged in areas that match our natural preferences, we tend to be excited, in flow, and progress comes easy for us. When we're stuck in areas that don't match our preferences, it's harder for us to get engaged and energized. If we're not aware of what's going on, we may cut corners or go too fast.

Preference vs. Skills

Before we go further, it's important to distinguish the difference between preferences and skills:

Preference is about what we do naturally and enjoy doing most.	**Skills** are what we're trained to do and what we've learned, regardless of our preferences.

In our personal and professional lives, we use four types of thinking to solve problems and we can be good at all of them, regardless of our preferences.

Let's go back to the small fashion company I mentioned in Chapter 2 who had frustration with the team.

It turned out that Ruth had a very different way of thinking compared to her co-founder, Angela, and the other team members. As they worked together, each of them made assumptions about how the other team members were thinking. They would get frustrated when they found the rest of the team was thinking or doing things differently than they would. Team members were all very pleasant to each other, but these differences were creating an underlying tension that none of them fully recognized nor understood.

The New Golden Rule for Team Innovation

My recent TEDx talk, *The New Golden Rule for High Performance Collaboration*, challenged the traditional golden rule of "Do unto others as you would have them do to you." I suggested a new golden rule instead: "See others for who they are and embrace our diversity of thinking."[33]

Using the FourSight® assessment,[34] we were able to highlight issues related to the team dynamic:

- Ruth preferred ideating and implementing. She was the visionary leader who was constantly bringing new ideas to the team and encouraging them to make things happen quickly. Because the team also had a high preference for implementation, they were quick to take the ideas forward.

- Angela preferred clarifying. She often asked questions to ensure the team had enough data to move forward.

- It was challenging for Angela to be heard, as Ruth and the team all had low preferences around clarifying thinking.

- The team discovered that their most likely innovation pattern was to simply take an idea that seemed promising (regardless of whether that was in strategy) and begin to implement it, without taking time to thoroughly develop the concept, consider alternatives, or test them. As a result, their rate of failure was somewhat high, which affected the company's bottom line, since they were launching products that failed in the market (as opposed to failing early and cheaply as we describe later).

---

[33]Cahen, H. (2021). *The new golden rule for high performance collaboration* [Video]. TED https://www.ted.com/talks/helene_cahen_the_new_golden_rule_for_high_performance_collaboration.
[34]FourSight®. *Team Assessment*. FourSight® https://www.foursightonline.com/team-assessment.

Once Ruth and Angela realized this, we created processes to ensure they allotted enough time to ask questions and get data upfront, as well as developing and testing new ideas with customers. New steps in the process included sharing their ideas very early on by showing drawings or quick mock-ups of their new concepts to customers on a Zoom call, and have them react before they spend time and money creating 3D prototypes. They also made sure to listen to Angela's clarifying questions to gather more data as they started new initiatives and to check on possible answers to these questions, avoiding staying on the problem too long (which can be a downside of working with people with a clarifying preference). They began to see the value Angela brought, rather than being annoyed at her for slowing down the process and asking too many questions.

The team was now able to understand each other's different ways of thinking. They started to appreciate each person's unique contribution, and they were better able to leverage individual preferences in deciding roles and ways to work together. Ruth and Angela were able to lead in a more meaningful way, by providing guidance and focus in areas that the team may not have considered before.

This saved a lot of time, kept the team engaged, and led to more long-term success.

**Remember:
It's not about being right or wrong or fixing anything. Awareness allows you to build on strengths and improve.**

Example of FourSight® Individual Preference Profile

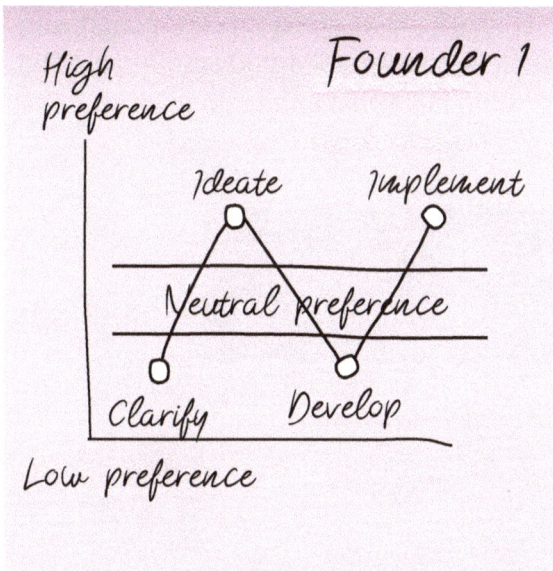

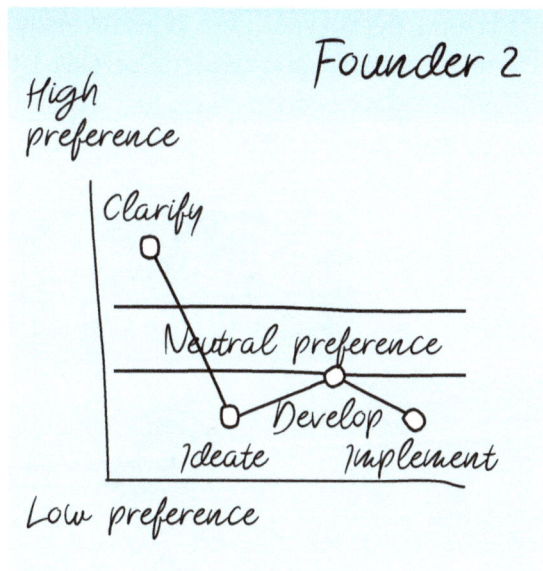

Founder 1

High preference — Ideate, Implement
Neutral preference
Low preference — Clarify, Develop

Founder 2

High preference — Clarify
Neutral preference
Low preference — Ideate, Develop, Implement

FourSight® Team Profile

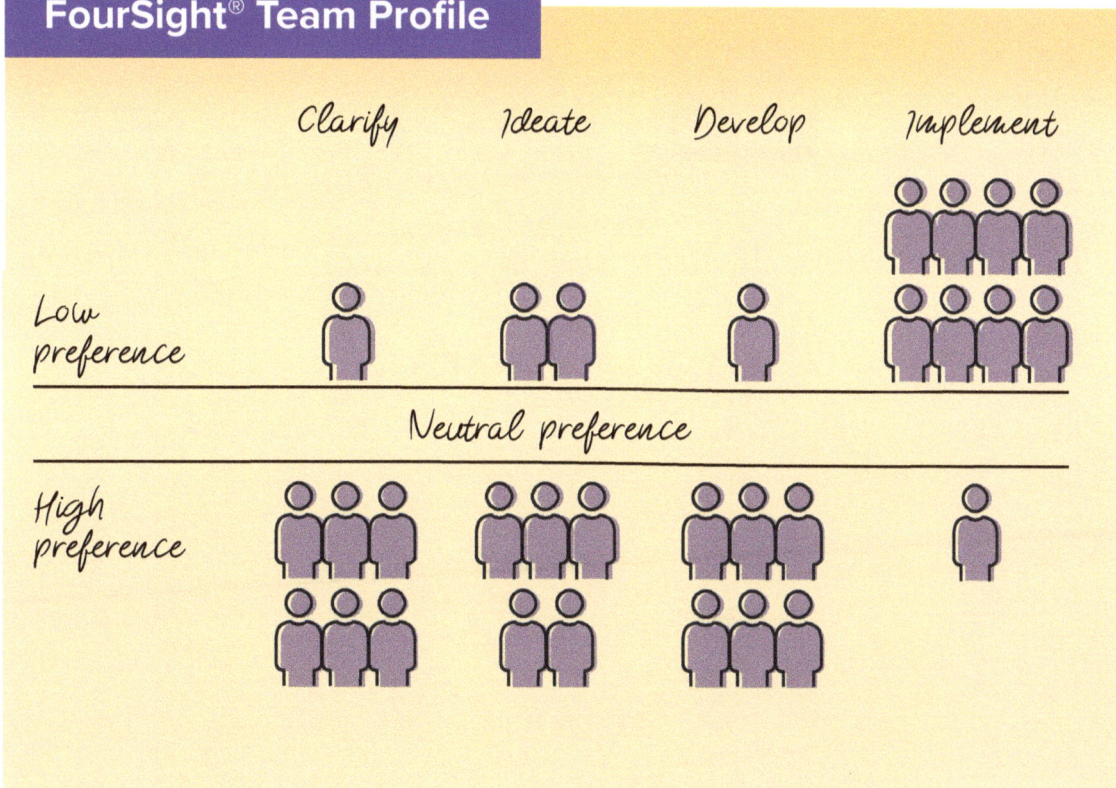

Clarify | Ideate | Develop | Implement

Low preference
Neutral preference
High preference

No Right or Wrong Ways of Thinking

It's important to be clear that there's no one right or wrong way to think—just *different* ways of thinking. Even if your team lacks diversity of thinking in some areas (as can happen when a team is formed based on technical skills), that can be fine. The IBM study of internal teams previously mentioned showed that awareness of the individual and team thinking profile can by itself make a difference in the outcome of a team.[35]

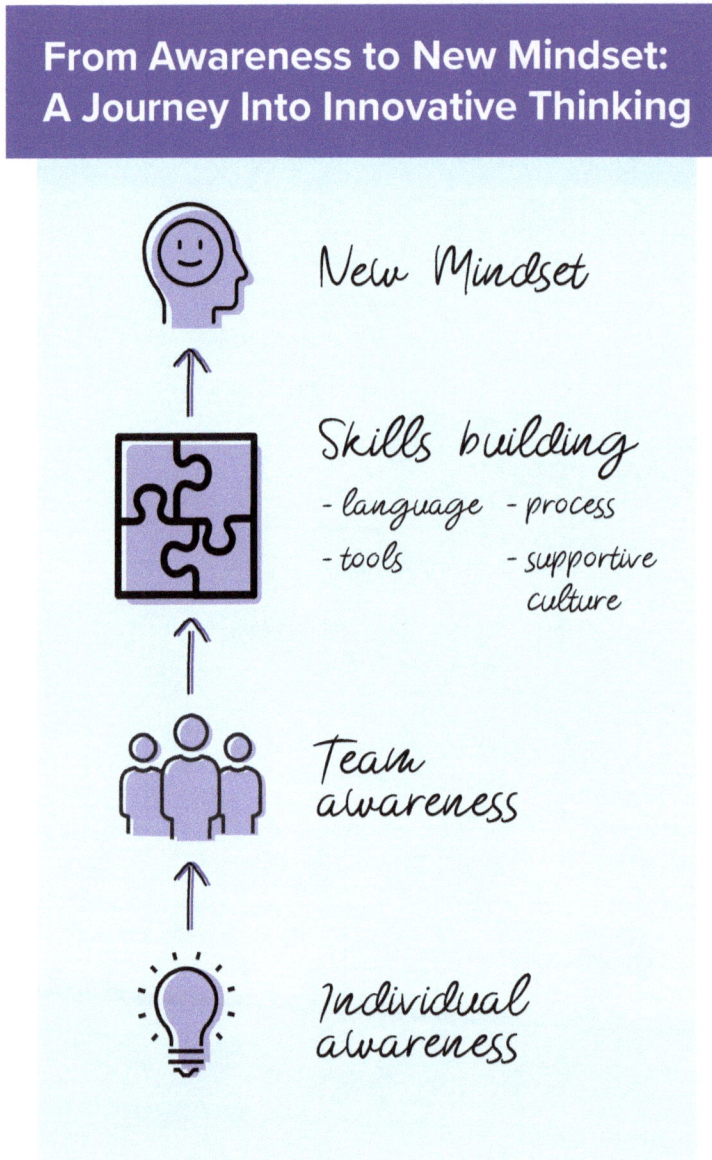

From Awareness to New Mindset: A Journey Into Innovative Thinking

New Mindset

Skills building
- language   - process
- tools   - supportive
              culture

Team awareness

Individual awareness

---

[35]DeCusatis, C. (2008). Creating, Growing and Sustaining Efficient Innovation Teams. *Creativity and Innovation Management*, 17(2), 155-164.

Awareness of Thinking Biases Exposes Blind Spots

Once a team understands each member's preferences and thinking profile, it's like a light switch has been flipped. Team members can now see previously hidden blind spots and address them through process development and skill building.

Being part of a team of people trying to solve problems without a clear, expressed, and shared set of processes, tools, and language creates frustration and inefficiencies. Sharing these goes a long way to achieve better results.

Think about how long you spent in school learning "technical" skills and general skills that you probably rarely use. In contrast, you probably spent very little time—if any—learning how to solve problems that require innovative solutions. It's likely that you were taught that problems have a right and wrong solution (think about math or physics challenges). You may have been pressed to argue your point of view and present arguments (think English or philosophy), or to solve technical challenges (working as an engineer, biologist, marketing manager, or finance specialist), or learned some scientific methods (doing scientific research). There was likely very little time devoted to simply learning processes to solve problems with others of different backgrounds, jobs, and specialties.

At best, you might have had a class in grad school (such as creativity for engineers, or system thinking). This was probably considered soft skills or "fluff" by some of your peers. And yet, these are the most useful skills one needs to become a strong contributor and work with others efficiently to solve the challenges required to stay relevant in a constantly changing world.

When I was coaching an MBA class related to solving problems, a student told me she was planning to work in banking, and was wondering why she would ever need to learn to innovate. I suggested that even in a traditional industry like banking, if she wanted to have a job five to ten years in the future, she should be learning about collaborating around innovation. Look at all the challenges and innovations we've seen in the fintech industry over the last decade or so!

Practice #3:
Observing Diversity and Its Impact in Meetings

Next time you are in a meeting with a team, observe and take notes about the following:

The ways diversity (of any type) helped in the meeting are

The challenges diversity brought to the meeting were

I saw tension or conflict when

The key underlining issues were

I observed my own biases when

I saw myself being frustrated when

Next time, I can help support diversity of thinking by

Chapter 4

Gathering Around the Fire: *Supporting Collaborative Diverse Teams*

As a trained facilitator, I know that creating effective collaboration requires a level of thinking that is often invisible to the groups with whom I work. However, thoughtful thinking and planning can make a huge difference in creating trust, enabling all voices to be heard, and ensuring the team is fully engaged.

Establishing a consistent process with established tools supports all ways of thinking and improves collaboration. Each person doesn't have to advocate for their own way of solving a problem. The team can go through the steps required and use tools that may help each member access the thinking required for the specific task at hand. Having a common approach helps everyone to be on board and focus on the content. The process is completely transparent and an enabler, rather than a source of discussion and resistance.

People often ask me how I deal with conflict when working with teams. First, I would like to define conflicts in opposition to debates using the Ekvall definition from his organizational climate research. Conflicts includes "the presence of personal and emotional tensions" while "debates" involve "the occurrence of encounters and clashes view-points, ideas and differing experiences and knowledge." In his research, Ekvall showed that while debates (in addition to other eight dimensions) support creativity and innovation in organizations; conflicts are the only dimension that negatively affects them.[36]

Conflict is usually quite limited in my work, because of the way we set up processes and use the right tools to create a climate that is supportive to creativity and innovation. Here are the key principles:

- **Start with clear, shared, and explicit criteria.** So when you move to decision making, there will be less subjectivity. It's not about what alternatives you like, but which ones best meet the criteria (see page 77).

- **Give everyone a voice.** At least in the diverging phases, using sticky notes is a great equalizer. Everybody can write as many notes as possible, and it's mostly anonymous so there's less attachment to "my thought, my idea." When shared, this becomes a collective piece of work.

- **No surprises.** When the process and tools are known in advance, everyone can focus on outcomes and content, which avoids friction related to differences in cognitive styles. Having a clear process, agenda, and timing goes a long way in avoiding worries about not being able to share your thoughts, while allowing everyone to contribute.

- **Be clear on the decision process.** There's no right or wrong answer, but clear communication is key to avoiding disappointment. Be upfront as to whether the decision making will be made unanimously, by the majority, later by management, or in some other way. The worst situation for a team is to think they are the decision maker and to realize later that actually management will make a decision regardless of their work. (This is particularly distressing if the managers were not involved in the teamwork.)

---

[36]Ekvall, G. (1996). Organizational Climate for Creativity and Innovation. *European Journal of Work and Organizational Psychology*, 5(1), 105–123.

The Importance of Empathy

I define empathy as the ability to understand and share the feelings of another. It's an important element of design thinking, often viewed as externally focused (for understanding your users), but it's also important as an internally focused principle.

We want to apply empathy towards our colleagues, teammates, and others with whom we work in order to understand their background and what challenges (both professional and personal) they may be facing. It's critical when working in collaborative teams that we bring our whole selves to our work.

We think we can compartmentalize, yet the person who shows up for work is the same person who struggles with childcare, suffers the loss of a parent, or has other personal challenges. Particularly in the post-COVID era, we see how these aspects of our lives are so connected. Being in a virtual or hybrid meeting makes this even harder, as we don't have the informal conversations before and after in-person meetings where we can share these other parts of our lives with others.

> **It's critical when working in collaborative teams that we bring our whole selves to our work.**

Here's a check-in exercise that will help a group get a feel for what's going on with each team member. At the beginning of a meeting, ask each individual to pick a color that describes how they feel. Make it explicit that this does not have to be about work. Have each person share their color and, if they are willing, explain why.

Or, ask them to choose a number from 1 to 10 to describe how they feel and then to explain why they made that choice. Then, go back and forth with people with the highest numbers, then the lowest numbers, ending with the middle 5 to 6—always asking why they feel that way.

Another version used by a VP of a pharmaceutical company with their team is called "Tune-up." Each member answers the question, "What do I bring today with me in this meeting today?" Answers might be, for example, that I'm frustrated because my car broke down, or that I'm waiting for a phone call from my child about whether she has been accepted at the university she hopes to attend.

As simple as these exercises seem to be, they're really helpful for people to share. This allows them to be more present and to have more empathy and understand why a colleague may be frustrated, disengaged, or critical. More often than not, it may have little to do with the work situation at hand.

■ The Performance Team Equation

$$(D + DT) \times (P + T) \times C = PT$$

(Diversity + Diversity of Thinking) x (common Process + shared Tools) x supportive Climate = Performance Team

I've created this equation as a way to highlight the importance of both the **diversity** of people and thinking, and the **commonality** of process and tools. This is critical when working with a diverse group, as well as in an overall supportive environment. Too often, these dimensions are not thought about together. We may promote diversity without acknowledging that we need to find efficient and collaborative ways to work together. Or, we might promote a process without acknowledging that the outcome will be optimized with a diverse team. Finally, the culture needs to be supportive of work situations where there may be uncertainty and failure.

Let's examine each of the elements of this equation.

D: Diversity

All types of diversity are critical to innovation teams to allow us to raise assumptions and biases, and to build outcomes based on multiple perspectives. Diversity in itself won't create innovation or change. A diverse group of people may have a harder time working together (since it's easier to be and work with people "like us"), UNLESS they're aware of what that diversity entails and they embrace it.

DT: Diversity of Thinking

As mentioned before in Chapter 3, understanding and acknowledging that we have different preferences in the way we solve problems and valuing that difference will help teams work better, avoid conflicts, and allow people to contribute further.

P: Process

A clear and shared process goes a long way toward improving performance. It should be differentiated from the content; otherwise, the blurring makes it hard to solve conflicts and differences when they arise. For example, people may not realize whether they are fighting for their idea (content) or because they feel unheard (process issue):

- **Content** is focused on what the group needs to discuss, the outcomes, and who should be involved in the meeting.

- **Process** is about how to achieve the meeting goals in an efficient, participatory way through agenda-building (including selecting the best time and process for each part of the meeting), meeting facilitation (focusing on achieving the agenda, regardless of the content, as well as managing flow of information, time, and issues as they arise), and people management for optimum participation and input.

While there are many processes that can be used (I personally like to use my own, a mix of FourSight® and Design Thinking), what is most important is to use a process with which all team members are familiar (and, ideally is one in which they have training), so the process is an efficient enabler that allows the content to emerge in a faster and conflict-free way.

T: Tools

Once there's a shared process (think about an understanding of how we build a house), the tools help make the process work in a more efficient way, and address specific steps and tasks (see Chapters 5 and 6).

C: Climate and Culture

As I often remind my clients, you can have the best team and process, but if the organization culture (that is, its values, what's acceptable or not) or climate (Is it a positive place? Are we inferring blame when people make mistakes?) is not supportive, you will kill innovation very quickly.

P: Performance Teams

The outcome of this equation is the potential for a team to be flexible, collaborative, and able to work together in an efficient way when creating innovative outcomes and change.

How to Make This Equation Successful

1. Clear roles and responsibilities, particularly of management and the facilitator

When content and process blur, too often we blame failure on the team, their limited knowledge, or a lack of collaboration. But it may simply result from being unaware of their differences and ways that process can enable success. Often, the roles around process leadership are not clear. The common assumption is that the manager or the person calling the meeting has to be the facilitator. That's why it's so important to know the roles on a team (just like on a sports team) and to decide who should be in the room (or not).

> **To schedule, prepare, manage, and facilitate successful meetings and collaborative work, you need BOTH content and process.**

Here's a perspective of a VP working with a large team:

"Maybe the role of the manager as part of the innovation is something to explore on its own right. Personally, when I believe some team members won't see me just as one of the team for a specific exercise, I prefer to opt out, with the personal price for me to accept the outcome. A practical example: My organization has stopped asking me my opinion on the branded name of a new product—they just inform me. I take comfort in the fact that the creative process is inclusive and has guard-railed to accept the result 'as is.'"

Ideally, when dealing with the type of complex issues often encountered with innovation projects, having a neutral facilitator and process expert who will focus on the process and leave the content to the team is the simplest and cleanest way to go. A neutral facilitator (either an external or internal consultant) will avoid the tension of having a team member (or, possibly worse, the manager!) being the facilitator.

This avoids the possibility of the facilitator overinfluencing the group because of their power or possibly introducing biases (consciously or not) to get ideas and recommendations adopted by the group. As a facilitator, a team member would need to be careful about sharing their own thoughts or opinions, and not participating in the discussion (or speaking last), to avoid the risk of overinfluencing the group and possibly creating mistrust and disengagement.

In addition, a facilitator who is also a content expert will have to manage the delicate balance of focusing on two very different tasks at the same time: ensuring the process is optimized and that the desired outcomes are reached.[37]

As a facilitator, I'm trained to see and understand that process and content are two very distinct elements, and that both are required for a successful meeting. To schedule, prepare, manage, and facilitate successful meetings and collaborative work, you need BOTH content and process.

2. Thoughtful Planning

Process is too often neglected. An agenda is put together very quickly. Facilitation roles are unclear. Time management is poor, so the meeting runs late, or some topics are neglected. The process for speaking is unclear. Outcomes are nonspecific or non-quantified. The full team may not be fully present when each person is speaking (with virtual meetings, multitasking and disengagement are very easy to do and often not apparent to the rest of the team). If you don't manage the meeting process, you may never get to the content, because the process (or lack thereof) is in the way.

Here's how to establish an effective process:

Start with a clear agenda and decision-making process

It's often assumed that the person calling the meeting will be in charge of the agenda, but this may or may not be the case. In my experience, there's often not enough time or thought put into the agenda and outcomes, decision-making process, and selection of tools and collaboration approaches to maximize collaboration efficiency, avoid conflict, and give each member a voice.

---

[37]Roger Schwarz's book is a great resource to help better understand the different roles and skills required for great facilitation and team collaboration. Schwarz, R. (2016). *The Skilled Facilitator (3rd ed.)*. Jossey-Bass.

If you are invited to a meeting without a clear agenda and outcomes, you may want to reconsider attending or step in to help!

Clarify who makes the decisions and how

While this may seem obvious, frustrations can easily develop if the group believes they are the decision makers, but that turns out not to be the case. Sometimes only a few people in the group or someone who isn't even part of the meeting will make the final decision—regardless of what the group recommends or decides.

There's no right or wrong way to make decisions, but clarity goes a long way. When I work with a group, I recommend having the decision makers in the room, as this makes the process more transparent and efficient.

The worst scenario is to have a decision maker say they want to empower the group to make the decision, not be a part of the meeting, and then afterward decide they disagree—changing the decision or disregarding the group's work. In my experience, this is the best way to make participants feel unappreciated and to lose momentum and energy around a project.

Reflection ———————————————————————

Think about how decisions are made in your organization. How clear is the decision-making process?

Do you remember instances where unclear decision making created frustration, conflict, and/or disengagement?

Clarify decision criteria

This is critical, yet often not discussed upfront. An unclear agenda, focusing on pushing the "right" idea or point of view, and using personal preferences to evaluate another participant's perspective and viewpoint can create conflict and frustration. The result is messy, inefficient, and ineffective decision making.

Wherever you may be in the process, decisions may have been made previously (or the team may think they were made) without in-depth discussions. It may be worth reviewing or summarizing to be sure the team is on the same page.

I always encourage the team (or management) either to provide the criteria for decision making upfront, or have the team create their own criteria at the beginning of a project. This goes a long way towards clarity, alignment, and easier decision making. Innovation projects have many areas of uncertainty and ambiguity, but clear decision-making criteria should be specified upfront—while acknowledging that criteria may have to change as the project progresses or more information becomes available.

For instance, we may think that being able to launch in six months is a key criterion, then discover down the line that it will actually take twelve months to launch. Or, the team may learn you can't meet all the criteria perfectly, and there's a trade-off to be considered: launching in six months with higher costs versus twelve months with lower costs and potentially better quality.

Ensure every participant has a voice

Use tools that will make this more efficient. If you have an hour meeting with ten participants, each participant will, on average, have six minutes to talk and 54 to remain silent. In a virtual call, that will be 54 minutes where it's easy for participants not to be fully present, to multitask, or simply to disappear totally for a while.

There are simple yet powerful tools and ways to organize a meeting to make it so much more efficient:

- Focus on interaction that can't be done asynchronously. Reviewing a report or getting initial feedback can easily and much more efficiently be done before a meeting.

- Share the agenda prior to the meeting. Be clear about pre-assignments and documents that are expected to be reviewed prior to the meeting. There's nothing more frustrating than being in a meeting where people show up uninformed, having not read the documents, or—even worse—make assumptions because they didn't do the pre-work. Anything that can be done offline asynchronously should be done that way.

- Give everyone a voice. This could be round-robin (with specific allotted time with), the ability to raise hands. Use the chat room in a virtual meeting or other visual tools.

- Use small group/breakout rooms as much as possible. In a group of three to five, everyone is involved. Either have groups work on the same topic and then report back to the larger group, or have groups work on different aspects of the same project, allowing for more efficient use of time.

Use visual ways to collectively collaborate

Flip charts, butcher paper, or virtual white boards and moveable notes in a common space are all great ways to work together with many benefits:

- They are visual. Everyone can see the same information in one place.

- They allow work in parallel—rather than one by one, as in a conversation. Use sticky notes or virtual notes, where each member can write down their thoughts at the same time.

- **They are more inclusive.** Role/power dynamics are not as important (since everything can be posted, and no one has to know who posted it). Different styles are heard (quiet, more introverted people have an equal chance to be able to post as more vocal and extroverted ones). This also eliminates the hierarchy (you may not know where a thought comes from) and fighting for "your ideas," ensuring that more junior or less assertive people have an equal chance to be part of the process.

- **They help visual thinkers.** This allows information to be captured, as well as to be easily moveable and "clusterable" see more tools around clustering in Chapter 6.

- **They facilitate asynchronous work.** This is particularly true with virtual white boards. In addition, they make it easy to keep track of progress in one place. Information can be continuously added prior to or after the meeting, or by people that can't attend. This is great for international teams, where time differences make it hard for everyone to contribute in real time. It's also helpful for people who want or need time to think about the work outside the time allocated for meetings.

- **They create a virtual "war room."** In the past, large organizations had "war rooms" with all the information for a project hanging on a wall of a room dedicated to the project, and everything in one place. Now, the team can use virtual boards to go back and revisit as the project moves along and it's easier than scrolling linearly through information on Slack or other document management programs. With virtual boards, you can have as many rooms as you want and keep the project up as long as needed.

- **They are portable.** You can easily move the information around, cluster it, prioritize or vote on it, build on it, etc.

---

3. Making the environment safe and supportive

It's important to make it safe for people to experiment—to build an environment where people can come up with things and fail without being beaten up. Team members should be able to be themselves—to express their perspective, creativity, and their own way of thinking. And sometimes that may mean deciding who should be or not be in the room (particularly whether upper management may help or inhibit the work). In the next chapter, we'll go into details on the concept of diverging, but for now consider the power of simply suspending judgment for both you and the group. Asking a team to do that and give themselves time to imagine "what if," even for a short moment, will build trust that even crazy thoughts are acceptable, and the group is willing to consider all possibilities, rather than shutting them down.

> **How management reacts and supports or dismisses the team is critical to the success of innovation. Even when a project is stopped, that doesn't mean it's a group failure.**

In addition, the role of leadership is critical in creating a safe environment for innovation. At the end of the day, there will be a decision by management to evaluate the work of the team and decide whether or not to move forward. How management reacts and supports or dismisses the team is critical to the success of innovation. Even when a project is stopped, that doesn't mean it's a group failure. To the contrary, it may be the right decision, and lessons can be learned from this that are valuable to the organization. Postmortem debriefing and celebrating failures (and successes) go a long way to create a safe environment to innovate.

Large organizations, in particular, can easily squash innovation (because they're worried about taking risks), so one way to alleviate this is to have a project champion—a high-level manager who will protect the team from early criticism or be the spokesperson to upper management. It provides a wall for the team that enables them to focus for a while on the task at hand rather than navigating the politics of the organization. In my experience, it's often best if this person is not involved in day-to-day activities, but provides a sounding board and a coaching role to the team. It's also important that they're kept updated and brought onboard at key critical times so they can decide how and when to best communicate with upper management. This provides a safety net to the team.

Reflection ————————————————————————————————————

Think about a project on which you worked:

• *If you had a team champion, how did this make a difference?*

• *If you did not have one, how do you think a champion might have made a difference?*

Practice #4:
Meeting Management

Think about a meeting in which you're going to participate, or, ideally, one you will lead.

Spend at least 30 minutes thinking about the best way to facilitate the meeting, including:

- List of attendees: Who should really be there and why?

- Preparation work: What should the attendees do before the meeting?

- Agenda:
  - Outcome for the meeting
  - Agenda items (including opening and closing) with timing, responsibilities, and outcome for each section
  - Ways to facilitate (the process you will use): Open discussion, round-robin, small group work, reporting format, etc.

- At the end of the meeting, take five minutes for feedback by asking people:
  - What did you like? What worked?
  - What concerns do you have?
  - How might we better manage our time in the future?
  - What suggestions do you have for future meetings?

Alternatively, you can use the POINt tool (on page 110).

After your meeting, reflect on the following, making the distinction between process and content:

What I liked about the meeting and how I acted is (content/process): ....

....

....

Here's what was challenging for me (content/process): ....

....

....

Next time, I'd like to do this better (content/process): ....

....

....

Chapter 5

Building a Fire That Lasts: *Principles of Applied Innovation*

Now that you have a sense of why diversity of thinking is important, you should start being more aware of the ways we think differently, and how we can bring different ways of thinking to the innovation process.

So, what's next? Think back to the Performance Equation (see page 57). We've discussed how people think differently; now it's time to focus on the innovation process.

A shared process and tools make you freer to focus on content in a more efficient and conflict-free manner. In my work, I rarely encounter people who complain about having to deal with conflicts on their teams because of the approach I use.

Having a shared process and language can make the hidden/implicit part of the thinking process explicit, so that everyone can participate and contribute. This allows the team to build common skills—regardless of individual preferences—which in turn makes team members feel more comfortable in all types of activities and tasks.

This is most helpful for those areas that are out of our personal preferences, as we may not think about or know how to tackle this part of the work. Imagine you have a low preference for generating ideas. For example, your natural tendency may be to take one idea and move it forward quickly. By learning the importance of ideation, you'll be more likely to feel comfortable generating a series of ideas, as well as understanding why this exercise can create better outcomes.

Processes for innovation are found under many names: Design Thinking, Lean Thinking, TRIZ, Six Sigma, Agile, Creative Problem Solving, and others. Some of these are more focused on incremental change and measuring output, while others are more about broader innovation. As we described in Chapter 2, at the highest level, there's a universal creative process that includes steps we can take to get unstuck and solve a new challenge:

Understand the challenge you're facing.

Come up with ideas to solve it.

Develop these ideas into solutions, build prototypes, and test them.

Implement.

The way we naturally think about solving a problem (**our thinking**) can also be used as a systematic **process** to innovate and create change. By simply making the **process** explicit and adding the correct tools, we become more collaborative.

This is likely to be an iterative process (which is reflected in this version of the model). Expect to learn and fail along the way, as you continue improving and innovating. Sometimes, the back-and-forth is a series of mini steps, as there's a need to fine-tune an area. Other times, we have to go back to the drawing board and start back at defining the problem (if it turns out we are solving for the wrong one!). Be sure to understand and assess where you are in the process and what needs to be done on an ongoing basis.

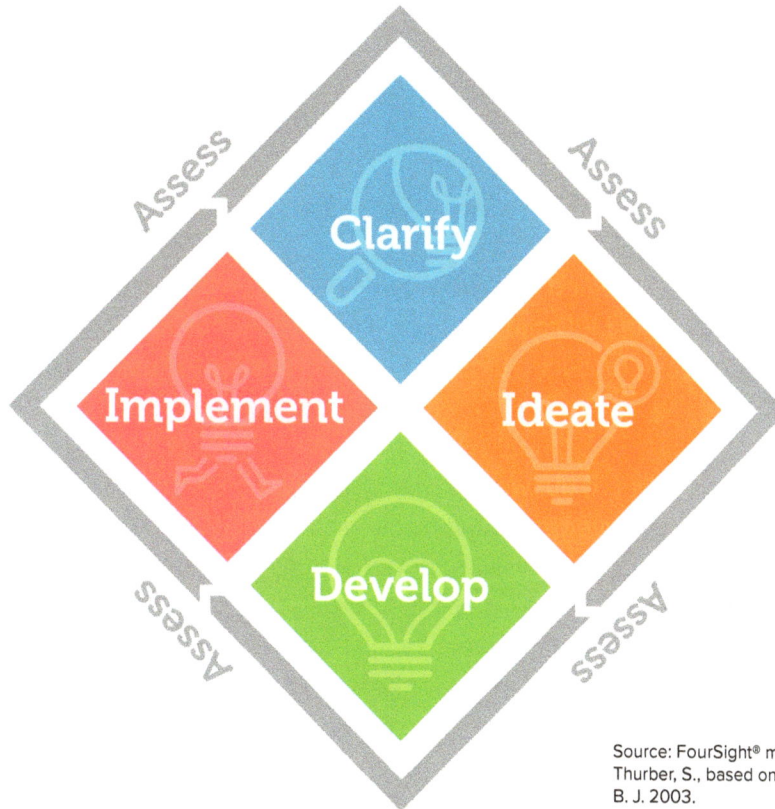

Source: FourSight® model: Nielsen, D., Thurber, S., based on Puccio, G. J., Miller, B. J. 2003.

Before we get into the concepts and tools that can help you collaborate, let's spend a moment thinking about how tools are best used.

Just as you need to understand how to build a house before learning about the tools you might use, there are four key building blocks to a successful process:

- The dynamic balance of creativity and associated rules
- The use of notes (virtual or real)
- The importance of success criteria
- Managing the group dynamic to empower everyone to participate

While AI tools may be useful to get some of the information (for instance suggesting a list of ideas), understanding these building blocks is still critical.

ⓘ Solving the Right Problem

GE Healthcare wanted to find new ways to help children be more comfortable when getting an MRI scan. An MRI scan can be a scary experience for a child because they need to stay immobile for a long time, even as the machine emits a continuous loud, banging noise.

Rather than trying to figure out ways to decrease the noise, the team figured out that the problem was about integrating the noise in a way that was less threatening. They came up with the concept of creating an adventure for the child. The MRI machine became an exploration vessel—a pirate cruise, a jungle trek, or an underwater expedition. This made the children feel special and excited about participating in this activity. In many cases, it even eliminated the need for anesthesia. Children were now enthusiastic about the process, and the staff no longer had to spend considerable time calming and reassuring them before undergoing this important test.[38] This limited stress for both the patient and staff, and saved time and money.

■ The Four Key Building Blocks

1. The Dynamic Balance (or Creative Breathing)

Often, we think that creativity is about generating many options (particularly a lot of ideas), but it's much more than that. *If you take away just one idea from this book, please make it this one!*

Creativity is a succession of first generating possible options, which we call **diverging**, then selecting and narrowing down options, in a process we call **converging**. Think of this as the **breath of creativity**.

---

[38]Birss, D. (2022). *Friction Co-Author Interviews GE Healthcare Designer on Innovative MRI Design for Young Children* [Video]. YouTube. https://www.youtube.com/watch?v=QCKSx3yMC34.

When you diverge and generate options (*breathing in*), you want to suspend judgment and generate as many options as possible.

When you converge (*breathing out*), you want to be systematic and decide which of these options you'd like to consider moving forward, based on a set of agreed-upon criteria.

Both of these activities are creative and critical to successfully moving through the innovative process. **Here's what's key: You can't do both at the same time!** Just like when you breathe, it's impossible to inhale and exhale at the same time.

This is where we often fail. As soon as someone comes up with a new thought, we immediately judge it, saying things like, "That will never work,'" "This idea costs too much," "That's very stupid," or, the infamous, "We've already tried that before." This premature judgment is likely to end the potential for something new and transformative to develop. And the worst voice of judgment is often our own (as we don't want to look stupid or silly or crazy), which stops us from even sharing our thoughts.

Diverging and converging activities can be found anywhere in the process:

> - You can generate many insights or significant data on a single problem, and you can also generate a long list of possible problems to solve. You can develop many ideas to solve any single problem, and just as many ways to develop and execute any one idea and test it. You can also list a number of different actions to take to implement and sell any specific idea.
>
> - Once you have created the options, you'll need to select and pick the one(s) you would like to move forward. In each of these situations, you'll need to consider the dynamic balance again and again while moving through your project.
>
> - The key is to leave time between the diverge and converge phases to give a chance to generate many options before you select. Like writing and editing, they should not be done together.

Dynamic Balance of Divergence and Convergence in Creative Thinking

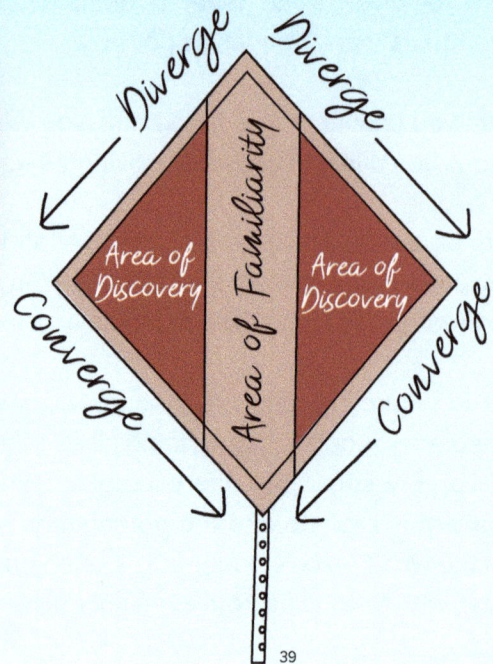

Diverge Diverge

Area of Discovery

Area of Familiarity

Area of Discovery

Converge Converge

39

TIP

Suspending Judgment

If you're in a meeting and people immediately rush to judgment (usually a negative one) when a new idea is shared, suggest to the group that for the next few minutes, we will all suspend judgment.

Set a time limit. During this time, everything will be heard without being judged. You'll know this means we're diverging, but you don't have to use the term. Then, later the team can evaluate the options in a systematic way (which is, of course, converging).

This also works when you're tasked with coming up with new options by yourself. Suspend your self-judgment even for a few seconds, and give those new thoughts a chance.

39Puccio, G. J., Murdock, M. C., & Mance, M. (2005). Current developments in creative problem solving for organizations: A focus on thinking skills and styles. *The Korean Journal of Thinking & Problem Solving, 15*, 4–79.

Practice #5:
New ideas

At your next meeting, notice what happens when someone introduces a new thought. Is it immediately shut down? Put aside for later? Simply ignored? Discussed immediately with pros and cons? Written down in a visible place as you look at different alternatives?

....
....
....
....

Notice what happens to the person who suggested the idea. How do you think they feel? How may this affect their behavior for the rest of the meeting?

....
....
....
....

If possible, ask them directly how they felt and how this may affect their future behavior.

....
....
....
....

Guidelines for Diverging and Converging

These guidelines are critical, yet rarely used (particularly the convergent guidelines!). They clarify the mindset needed for these activities to be successful. Here's a summary of the rules. Details are at the end of this chapter.

Creative Thinking Guidelines

Divergent Guidelines
Generate Options

- Defer judgment
- Strive for quality
- Seek wild & unusual ideas
- Build on other ideas
- Be visual

Convergent Guidelines
Select Options

- Be affirmative
- Be deliberate
- Check objectives
- Improve ideas
- Consider novelty

You're either diverging or converging . . .
Never do both at the same time.

[40]

[40]Based in Isasken & Treffinger (1985); Miller et al. (2001); Osborn (1963); and d.school for the "be visual" rule; Isasken and Treffinger for converging rules.

2. The Use of Notes (Real Sticky Ones or Virtual Alternatives)

Speaking one-at-a-time to solve problems and generate options is inefficient and often doesn't help those who have the hardest time speaking up in a group. Those who are new, have a lower hierarchical position, or are more introverted are unlikely to share their thoughts. This often has little to do with the quality and importance of their input. Note taking is tedious and often done after the meeting, therefore, not supporting the collective thinking process.

On the other hand, allowing for parallel thinking in a quiet environment where each person writes down their thoughts—either on physical sticky notes or virtual notes on a white board—gives everyone the same amount of time and equal importance. In a few minutes, you'll get X times more thoughts, where X represents the size of the group, compared to having discussions one person at a time.

Think of a white board. The beauty of notes (physical or virtual) is that they can be moved, clustered, and organized/reorganized to help patterns emerge or to prioritize.

You'll still need to spend time to sort out the thoughts, but at least they'll all be in one place. Those who are visual thinkers also find this is a much easier way to keep track of options.

TIP

Converging Can't Be Rushed

Converging takes more time than diverging, because you need time to discuss and evaluate options, then decide which to eliminate and put aside. A rule of thumb is that converging should take twice as long as diverging. So if you spend 30 minutes generating ideas, plan to spend at least an hour selecting which ideas to move forward.

3. Clear Criteria for Success

This seems like such a basic concept, but again and again I've seen teams struggle because they're not clear on what success looks like. Every time there's a need to select and eliminate options, this becomes a personal battle (with each person thinking they hope their idea wins!), rather than a more objective approach, where the whole team reviews options in the same way.

Sometimes it may also be because management puts the team in an impossible position when they want it all (high value product impact, easy to make, and the ability to launch quickly, for example), and it requires the team to get a better understanding of priorities and trade-offs so they can then take the most important criteria first, and then continue fine-tuning options using the next set of criteria. For instance, we want the product to make at least $3 million in the first year (#1 criteria), and within the possible options, we will work on those that can be the fastest to be launched (#2 criteria).

Agreeing on success criteria at the beginning of a project can make a major difference in the outcome. Every time the team will be converging and selecting where to focus and what to eliminate, they will have an objective way to evaluate options, rather than a subjective one (where picks are based on their own preferences).

> **Agreeing on success criteria at the beginning of a project can make a major difference in the outcome.**

Examples of Useful Project Criteria

- **Expected outcome**

- **Timing** (needs to be feasible/implementable within a defined framework)

- **Financial constraints** (cost no more than . . .)

- **Financial impact** (sales, revenue, return on investment, risk of cannibalization of other products/services . . .)

- **User impact** (Will it make the users life better? Easier? Cheaper? More joyful? . . .)

- **Other impact** (such as revenue, number of people impacted, return on investment, efficiency . . .)

- **Easiness** to make it happen

- **Level of risk** (including risk of not doing it which is often forgotten)

- **Level of satisfaction** (for different stakeholders)

- **Novelty**

4. Managing the Team Dynamic and Energy

Because people have different preferences for parts of the innovation process, it's likely that you'll see individual and group energy fluctuate, depending on the type of activities. When someone is doing activities that are in their area of preference, they're likely to be fully engaged and energized. But when they're involved with activities in areas of low preference (for example, spending time identifying many new ideas when this is not their forte), their energy and interest tends to drop.

When you reach an area of low preference for a group, people may be disengaged, impatient to move forward, question the process, or they may just act tired. They may not even know why, but once you're familiar with the process and tools, and you understand how to effectively facilitate meetings with diverse type of thinkers, you'll start to notice and feel this and find ways to keep the group engaged.

TIPS

Here are a few tips:

- **Use a break in the flow.** This could be as simple as stretching for a minute together, taking a bio or snack break, or taking a longer break sooner.

- **Introduce some fun activities.** Ideally, these can still be related to what you're doing.

- **Time your meetings.** When dealing in areas of low preference, choose times when people are more likely to be engaged (for example, morning, rather than after lunch or the end of the day).

- **Introduce variety.** Try new exercises, activities, or tools the group hasn't seen before.

- **Break it up.** Working in small groups makes it easier to be engaged.

How This Works Together:
Planning the Holiday Vacation

Remember in our first practice when we asked you to plan your next vacation in five minutes? Here's how the process might work if we had time to use a clear planning process.

First, decide on the "challenge" at hand. You may assume this would be just to plan the trip. But if you were to take the trip with a group of friends, you may discover along the way that their understanding of the trip is quite different from yours. Perhaps they love to be very active and wake up early, while you want to relax on the beach and have leisurely two-hour meals.

Start by having a discussion with your friends to understand the criteria they'd use to consider the trip worthwhile. This might include the activities they'd like, the budget, type of places they want to stay, length of the vacation, location, etc. Ask each person to describe their best vacation, then read blogs or interview people that have been to the location you're considering. This will help everyone agree on the real challenge.

Let's say you decide the challenge is to plan a trip to Mexico in early June where you can meet locals, learn about the music scene, and get some beach time— while staying within a set budget. This would be a very different experience than a trip to Yosemite that is focused on such outdoor activities as hiking and camping. I guarantee that spending the time to discover the real challenge will make your trip planning—and the trip itself—more likely to be successful. In fact, it will help you all understand how to better define success.

Once you've established these criteria, you can spend time thinking of vacation activities. You might make a list of ways you could learn more about Mexican music, for example. In my world, we encourage you to develop as many ideas as possible, rather than coming up with just one or two. Go for ten, 20—even 50.

Next, develop some of the selected ideas into solutions that you'd like to prototype. This phase is critical to having a successful adventure.

Say you decide you want to go camping as a way to stay on budget, but you've never done it before. Before planning a two-week camping trip in Mexico, it may be useful to prototype your idea and go camping with your friends for a night locally. See if you're all still getting along after that. Did you enjoy camping, or did you realize it hurts your back? How would the camping experience in Mexico differ from that in the US? How easy would it be to find the right camping equipment there?

Finally, you'll need to get all the details together before and during your trip. Once again, there's room to diverge (for example, there are multiple ways to travel from the US to Mexico). You can come up with different options for each day and decide which ones to pick. Once you're in Mexico, you'll still need to look at options for each day (where to go to lunch, which beach to go to, what modes of transportation are available to get you to the beach, etc.), plan them, and make them happen. This process is a life process, often done without awareness. Being more aware of it can help make it easier, faster, and less likely to bring conflicts, so the adventure is so much better.

TIP

Choose What's Necessary

You may not need to review all four parts of the process each time. For instance, if you're going to visit your parents and you're taking the same trip as last year, you can just move to execution: Who's getting the tickets? Which day do we want to leave? Should we rent a car?

Practice #6:
Create your own learning

Review this chapter and pick one idea that inspires you. Apply to your personal or work situation and reflect on what you learned.

When I did

....

I noticed

....

....

The impact was

....

....

....

In the future I would like to try to (do more/less/differently/change)

....

....

....

....

■ Guidelines for Diverging and Converging

Diverging guidelines

Defer judgment	Acknowledge that when we have a thought, we shouldn't judge it immediately. When you're diverging, everything goes. The first step is to suspend our own judgment, as we often censor ourselves before sharing thoughts with others. When we're in diverging mode, we must accept that there's value in any thought that comes to mind, because it may be a new beginning. While it's very unlikely to be the final answer, it can still trigger new thoughts in yourself and others that may be of help to move the process forward. There's also value to a "brain dump." Getting rid of the obvious thoughts by writing them down and sharing them will force your brain to find new thoughts.
Strive for quantity	Research around ideation has shown that the more ideas are generated, the more *good* ideas are likely to emerge. Our mindset is that quantity drives quality. When we think quantity, that means a very large number. I usually suggest groups try to generate a hundred or more ideas. They often look at me like I'm out of my mind. However, well-facilitated work with a group of eight to ten participants can easily generate more than 200 ideas in less than an hour. This also means you'll need significant time to sort them out (see the tip below) and narrow them down. Going for quantity is also useful when you're trying to understand a problem (have we considered all the problems?), to look at data from many different angles, or to find new ways to implement your ideas (as the most obvious ways may not be best).

Seek wild and unusual ideas

This is connected to the first two points. If you're looking for innovation and change, it's likely that the easy, obvious ideas have already been considered and are not going to be the innovations you need.

Build on other ideas

Innovation is a team sport. Whether you work together in parallel or asynchronously, it's likely that the thoughts of other team members may help you make new connections and come up with more options.

Be visual

I find this hard for many groups to understand, as we are so accustomed to using words to describe our thoughts. And yet, as the popular saying suggests, a picture is worth a thousand words. Often, a concept can be better explained and shared using a visual rather than words. This doesn't have to be professional quality artwork. A quick hand-drawn sketch will usually suffice at this stage.

Converging guidelines

Guidelines for converging are generally less known than those for diverging. They're rarely used, because convergent activities are often ignored or minimized. Too often we move immediately to the ineffective technique, "Let's just vote." Yet, since converging is so critical to the success of the innovation process and takes more time, it should be given a major role. If you are in person, it's useful to post these rules on the wall of a meeting room or distribute them to team members ahead of the meeting if you're working remotely.

Be affirmative	Consider positives first, rather than going directly to the negatives.
Be deliberate	Give each option a chance to be examined fairly (using the criteria) without introducing your own biases.
Check your objectives	Often, we get sidetracked and forget our initial purpose. It's important to evaluate against that purpose. It's even better to have criteria for success set up front.
Improve ideas	Because we're in an iterative process, we should be flexible. As we're selecting options, new thoughts may come up. Consider these as well, rather than rejecting them because they weren't on the initial list. Or, as you evaluate an idea or thought, you may find new ways to refine it, strengthen it, or combine it with others.
Consider novelty	It's easy to forget that we're here to innovate and create change. Group decisions can be very conservative. If the group is uncomfortable with risk, it may end up selecting the most obvious and easy ideas, which often lack innovative potential. Remember what you're trying to accomplish. Be willing to take risks and move novel thoughts forward—even if they end up being reworked and fine-tuned later.

The Design Thinking Model

While earlier we reviewed FourSight® as a basic process describing the main steps to solve problems, I found that combining these steps with some key principles and tools coming from the Design Thinking world is very useful. While the design thinking overall approach is somewhat similar, it includes more explicit emphasis on:

• Being "user-centered" and cultivating empathy through the use of ethnographic research.

• The focus on the development of prototypes and iterative testing.

There are many variations on design thinking, but here is a teaching model that I found useful to understand steps and focus.

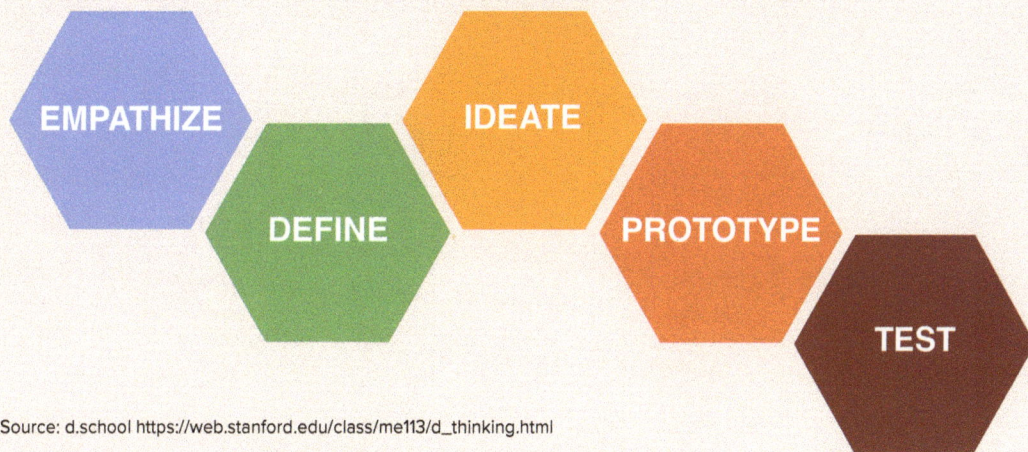

EMPATHIZE   DEFINE   IDEATE   PROTOTYPE   TEST

Source: d.school https://web.stanford.edu/class/me113/d_thinking.html

In this model:

• *Empathize* focuses on understanding your users using ethnographic research techniques, as well as secondary research/market research to help you *Define* the challenge (which corresponds to the one *Clarify* step in the FourSight® model).

• *Ideate* is similar in both models.

• *Prototype and Test* in the design thinking model are similar to *Develop* in FourSight®, with more emphasis on user-centered tools of development that are *Prototyping and Testing*.

• There's no *Implement* phase in this model, as it focuses more on the early stage of innovation.

Chapter 6

Sustaining the Warmth: *The Basic Toolbox*

Now that you understand the basic thinking steps and concepts involved in innovation and creating change, here are a few simple tools you can use to help you through the process. Before we get into the details, there are two basic principles to remember—no matter what tool(s) you use:

- **Remember to diverge first.** Then spend enough time converging, as you go through each phase of the process.

- **Establish success criteria upfront.** This will help you make better decisions as you move through the process. It will also help make sure everyone is aligned when it's time to converge.

When it comes to tools, less is more. Unless you are an expert facilitator and very familiar with the innovation process, having just a few simple tools with which you're comfortable is much better than bringing in a lot of tools that require advanced skills and practice, which distracts from the content. That's why I'm not a fan of books that focus only on tools. A tool is only as good as your understanding of how it works and how it can help.

With AI tools, you're likely to find many more options (such as identifying problems or ideas, giving you suggestions to implement, offering ways to cluster your ideas or rank them—even generating AI personas to test your concepts). I'd argue, though, that unless you really understand the underlying concepts around innovation, you are unlikely to be successful by leaving the process in the hands of an AI tool. After all, the same tools are available to all, and so the concepts are easier to generate for everyone. Your edge may rely in deeply understanding how innovation works.

> **Unless you really understand the underlying concepts around innovation, you are unlikely to be successful by leaving the process in the hands of an AI tool.**

Reading about a tool doesn't help you use it correctly—any more than reading about how to ski does not help you ski down moguls. In my work, I've learned about hundreds of tools, but I only regularly use five to ten of them. I am sharing here the ones I think are most important, yet simple enough. As with any new skills, you'll need to experiment and practice to become comfortable using the tools—particularly in a group setting. The tools suggested below comes from both the FourSight® and design thinking world and constitute my favorite basic toolbox. Some of these tools already exist with AI support, but understanding the tool in general is still relevant. I am not providing a list of AI version of the tools, as the field is evolving so quickly that the list will be irrelevant by the time this book is published. But my hope is that this will help you know what to consider.

Also, you may want to consider AI as a team member and one of the elements that can provide input (at this point, I would recommend also including human input in all the tools).

■ Tools for Clarification

I recommend three go-to tools in this part of the process: **5W&1H, Interviews and Observations**, and **Statement Starters**. Let's look at each.

5W&1H

The 5 W's are Where, What, When, Who, and Why.
The H is How.

This diagnostic tool is a great way to help you think through all the dimensions of your challenge. First, complete what you know, then identify areas where you need to learn more, get access to additional information, or talk to people who can help you understand this from a diversity of thinking, background, experience, and perspectives.

Take it one question at a time and use divergent thinking to get more than one answer. Ask the question, then ask the question again, adding **else** at the end: For example, When is the issue appearing? When else?

5W & 1H

a.k.a. Data Questions

Where? ....

What? ....

When? ....

Who? ....

Why? ....

How? ....

41

⁴¹Isaksen, S. G., & Treffinger, D. J. (1985). Creative Problem Solving: The basic course. Bearly Limited. *Noller, R. B., Parnes, S. J., & Bondi (1976). Creative actionbook. Scribner's Sons.*

Planning a Vacation Example—Using the 5W&1H

Here are some questions you may have asked your team when planning the Mexico trip we discussed earlier:

Where do we want to go?

When do we want to travel?

What activities to we want to do?

What budget do we have?

What activities do we want to try that we have not done before?

What is the best season to go?

What type of accommodations do we want?

Who is coming on the trip?

Why is this trip together important?

How can we meet local people and have a more authentic experience?

How can we get involved with the local music scene?

Interviews and Observations

We talked earlier about the importance of empathy (understanding others) as a critical skill in terms of embracing diversity of thinking. If I can't understand what motivates the other person, it's unlikely we can work together.

This same approach is useful as you try to identify a problem. It's important to understand the human approach. A key principle in design thinking is being **user-centered** or **human-centered**. For that, the best approach is to do **ethnographic research**.

Ethnographic research can apply to understanding any new environment. In a business context, it's useful to understand a situation in its complexity by looking at the interaction of people, objects, culture, understanding beliefs, behaviors, and attitudes.

This concept was first made famous by anthropologist Bronislaw Malinowsky in the 1920s, when he realized he couldn't simply use quick observations to understand the population he was studying. Malinowsky spent years living on various Pacific Islands, researching the indigenous populations to develop valuable insights.[42]

While Malinowsky was still very ethnocentric in his approach, the concept of observing and asking questions rather than making assumptions is a powerful one. In the past 30 years, it's started to be used by businesses and organizations. While it's not as thorough as what an anthropologist spending years with a specific population may do, the ethnographic approach has been adopted by businesses as a way to go deeper than traditional survey or focus groups, where you get information outside the real context, based exclusively on what respondents would report. An ethnographic approach can help all of us better understand a challenge by **observing and listening to the people who are directly impacted by the situation—in the real environment where they encounter it**. This is true whether that person is a consumer, a colleague, an expert, a supplier, or a friend.

Tom Kelley of IDEO wrote that, "If you are not in the jungle, you are not going to know the tiger."[43] No matter how much you read about tigers or watch movies about them, nothing will replace the experience of meeting a tiger in the jungle!

If you follow this simple, basic approach, you may learn more about a situation in a single hour than you could by spending years discussing it with your peers.

---

[42]Wikipedia https://en.wikipedia.org/wiki/Bronis%C5%82aw_Malinowski.
[43]Kelley, T. (with Litman, J.) (2001). *The Art of Innovation:* lessons in creativity from IDEO, America's leading design firm, p. 31. Doubleday.

The principles of ethnographic research are simple:

- **Observe and/or talk to the person in their natural environment.** Go to the jungle. This may be their office, their home, where they shop, or where they go for fun. It can be done virtually (which may even make it easier for someone to show you around their space).

- **Observe, ask, and listen.** Mostly, you should be observing and listening.

- **Anything in and about the setting is relevant information.** If you watch people eating dinner, observe what's on their plate but also how they eat, the pets that are around, the noise in the room, the neighborhood, the interaction, their move to and from the table, etc. Focusing just on what they're eating on their plate will miss the whole picture. Look at anything that might be interacting with the situation.

Let's say we want to interview a consumer about their use of a mobile phone app. Here's how we might approach this:

- Ask them to show us the various apps they have on their phones now, and to explain which one they use most and why (context). We could ask to see their statistics of time used on each app (as they may not realize where they really spend their time).

- Have them show us how they use the app we are researching and describe what they're doing while using that app.

- Ask them why they choose to use that app, what works, and what may be frustrating about it.

- Ask them to show us how they use their favorite apps.

- Ask them to show us an app that does *not* work well for them.

- Listen for the differences between what **they say they do and what they really do:** The gap between the two is a great source of information and potential for innovation. For example, they may say Facebook is easy to use, but they struggle to find a certain group or to locate a colleague with a common name to add as a friend.

- Conclude by asking if there were one thing they could change in that app, what would it be and why?

An Ethnography a Week Keeps the Assumptions Away!

Ethnographic research may seem intimidating, so let's simplify this further. Ethnography in the context of innovation should *not* be done by a specialized insights or user design department somewhere in your organization who produces a big report. Instead, consider having each member of your team take on one observational interview per person per month. Then, summarize what you've learned (ideally, do this as a group). Use the clustering technique (page 101). You'll be surprised how much you'll learn. The stories will stick, and as you create change, it will be easier to think about responding to the specific people you interviewed, rather than creating a broad description of an average group of users.

To get a more realistic and broader perspective about your challenge, get out of your own head. Check your facts, assumptions, and your biases. Consider your assumptions and even what you consider as "facts" as simple hypotheses until they are confirmed through research. This may help everybody feel less attached to them. Observe others interacting with your product or service, or simply watch them doing their job. Then, ask questions that will provide the diversity of perspectives critical to understanding the different aspects of your challenge. This will help you make a better decision about the exact problem you want to solve.

AI may offer persona or AI customers to test, but I believe there is something unique about being in the room with the person and seeing the connections of all elements, having the ability to use all our senses to make sense of what is happening for them, and mixing observation and discussion. The risk of AI is that we become more disconnected to our humanity and empathy, and ethnographic research is a way to anchor us. It is also possible that ethnographic research may be done through AI in the future, AI offering personas to make us understand human experiences. Either way ethnographic research is still a critical element to an innovation process.

Here are a few basic tips for conducting an effective interview:

TIP

- **Focus on the person you interview.** Assume you don't know anything. Ask questions, listen with compassion, and don't judge.

- **Ask questions in a neutral way.** Use unbiased open questions, rather than closed-end (yes/no questions).

  For example, ask:

  - *Can you tell me about your day? Rather than, How hard was your day (the assumption here is the day was hard) or, was your day hard (a yes/no question that will not provide insights)?*

  - *Can you show me how you use the app? Rather than giving them specific directions on how to use the app.*

  - *What do you think about this app? Rather than, do you like the app (yes/no)? Or, this is a great app, isn't it (introducing a positive bias that makes it hard for the person to contradict you)?*

- **Prepare an outline of the questions you want to ask.** Limit this to between six and twelve questions, but be flexible. If the person goes in an unplanned direction, you may find a nugget of information in an area you hadn't even thought about exploring.

- **Build trust.** Ask easy general questions first, then go to more specific inquiries.

- **Ask for examples, emotions, and stories.** These are more real and will provide better insights than general answers.

  Ask:

  - *Give me an example of a time . . . ?*
  - *What was the most frustrating experience you had . . . ?*
  - *How do you feel about . . . ?*

- **Remember, you are there mainly to listen.** You should not talk more than 15-20% of the time—at most.

I once taught basic ethnographic research to a group of executives. One of them decided to interview his colleague, who was a vice president in the same organization, but also had been his friend for years. On our call the following week, he explained how he learned more about his friend's challenges at work in just one hour of asking open-ended questions and simply listening than in ten years of working and hanging out together outside of work!

To get a more realistic and broader perspective about your challenge, get out of your own head. Check your facts, assumptions, and your biases.

Practice #7:
Ethnographic Research

In the next week or so, plan to do one piece of ethnographic research—an observation, an interview, or a combination of both:

- Schedule time with the person (ideally between 30 minutes and one hour).

- If you're going to observe, plan what you need to be watching and how you may document this (by taking notes, taking pictures, or recording videos, etc.).

- If you're conducting an interview, write your goals (what you're trying to learn). Prepare an outline of six to twelve questions (open-ended only). Decide how you will record the information (by taking notes, or using voice or video recording, for example). Determine what activities you may ask them to do (share pictures, show what they do on their phone or computer, explain how they use a product, show you their kitchen, closet, car trunk, etc.).

- Allow 30 minutes to an hour after to reflect on what you've learned and to create insights. Consider using the clustering tool below.

- Reflect on the process, using the POINt tool. See page 110.

Statement Starters

This is one of the simplest, yet most powerful tools available to clarify a challenge. Often, we create a long summary sentence about a challenge or vague goal, which does little to actually help us solve it. I could say, "I want to make a million dollars this year," but if I don't know how to make more money, or I have no time to devote to learning what to do—this is nothing more than a wish. It's a description of my goal, but not conducive to finding answers as to how to achieve it.

Statement starters are words that create an open challenge that you can then solve.

There are four we recommend:

1. How do . . . ?
2. How might . . . ?
3. In what ways might . . . ?
4. What may be . . . ?

Using statement starters forces you to do two things:

TIP

Take One Thing at a Time

You don't have to choose one single challenge. Sometimes you may decide there's more than one, but address them one at a time. This is less overwhelming than having a very broad problem to solve. Also, by having more specific questions, you can generate more innovative solutions. Using the principle of dynamic balance, consider generating several problem statements (diverging) before deciding which is the one you really want to solve (converging).

- **Ask a question.** By asking a question, your brain naturally will attempt to come up with solutions.

- **Focus on the area that needs solving.** In the previous example, there are many possible different challenges that could be solved: How to make a million dollars next year, how to make more money without feeling overworked and stressed out, how to live within my budget, what are all the ways I could have enough income to pursue my dreams?

Deciding which angle you want to use to tackle the challenge may bring you on a very specific path. Of course, in order to decide which challenge to solve, you first have to understand the different dimensions associated with the challenge (by doing ethnographic research and using the five diagnostic questions to guide you on the primary or secondary research you may need) before you can decide on which questions you want to focus.

Practice #8:
Generating Problem Statements

Think about either a personal or professional problem you'd like to solve.

Generate at least five to ten problem statements related to the problem using the statement starters. Pick the one you are most interested in solving.

#1 ....

#2 ....

#3 ....

#4 ....

#5 ....

#6 ....

#7 ....

#8 ....

#9 ....

#10 ....

I would like to work on: ....

....

■ Tools for Ideation

Brainstorming (for DIVERGING Only)

The most famous, most used (and also the most misused!) tool associated with creativity is brainstorming. There has been much controversy about this tool and whether it works or if it's now obsolete. I believe brainstorming is a great tool IF AND ONLY IF it's the right tool for the job (that is, you are trying to ideate and diverge on a clearly identified problem) and you know how to use it the correct way.[44]

Here's how to use brainstorming effectively.

Keys to Success:

☑ **Use sticky notes**, so everyone works at the same time. This is much more efficient, plus each team member has the same opportunity to generate options.

☑ **Give participants time to write down all their ideas before sharing.** This helps the introverts and people who may not feel comfortable fighting for airtime and gives everybody quiet time to think.

☑ When you share, simply **read each note without allowing any comments** (remember, we are in diverging mode).

☑ **Only one idea or piece of information per note**, so that notes can be moved and clustered later.

☑ **If some of the ideas are generated through AI help, add them to the mix**

This same process works virtually. All participants can write and post virtual notes at the same time.

---

[44]If you want to learn more about the controversy, check my blog post. Cahen, H. (2020). If I had a hammer. Strategic Insights. www.fireupinnovation/blog.

Steps:

▶ **Remind participants of the diverging rules**, especially that they must suspend judgment (including their own!).

▶ **Post the starting question or topic in a visible place**, so each person can see it for reference.

▶ **Give participants time to write down all their ideas or options** (one per note) silently for a few minutes.

▶ **Focus on quantity** at this stage, and give people a quota (for instance, ten minimum per person, or 200 for a group).

▶ Once everyone is done writing, **have each participant share their ideas aloud**, one at a time, then post them on a white easel sheet. For a virtual team, either have participants read their notes, or refer all participants to the virtual white board where they can see all the notes posted.

▶ **Decide if you want to do another round** of ideas and information:

  • Check your progress against your objective: Do you have enough options? Are they innovative enough?

  • If you want more options, trying using a different prompt to generate new ideas.

  • Look at the ideas already posted, and use them as inspiration for new ones.

  • Use a forced connection technique. For example, show a set of pictures or images and ask, "When you look at these pictures, what kind of new ideas do you have to solve the challenge?"

  • Challenge the group to come up with a couple of crazy ideas—options that they think the organization would never normally consider solving the challenge.

  • Consider using other ideation tools.

TIP

Brainstorming Doesn't Need to Happen in Real Time

Online brainstorming can also be done asynchronously. Give the group a few days to come up with ideas to solve the challenge. Have them post their notes on a virtual board whenever they want. This can be extremely effective, particularly with virtual or remote teams.

Affinity Diagram-Clustering: with or without Dot Voting

I was not joking when I mentioned you should be aiming for quantity! It's actually not difficult for a group of seven or more people to come up with 100–200 ideas in less than 30 minutes in a good brainstorming session. Now that you have a good list of new ideas, it's time to sort them and select them. Rarely is this done well, and that's why brainstorming gets a bad rap.

The most misused technique is voting, where a group votes to pick their top ideas—usually without clear criteria—under the false assumption that an idea written in 30 seconds will then be completely innovative and a winning solution—or no merit at all.

Think of this like planting seeds. An idea at this stage of the process is just a seed. You can't really tell by looking at it whether that seed will grow to become a beautiful tree or an ugly weed. But if you first sort your seeds into categories and try to better understand each group, you may decide that one particular category has a better chance of growing into the garden you would like to plant, or that at least some seeds in that group may be worth growing.

> **You can't really tell by looking at it whether that seed will grow to become a beautiful tree or an ugly weed.**

Clustering can be done with or without dot voting (which involves putting dots next to ideas that each person thinks are worthwhile). Instead of voting and deciding if each idea is good enough on its own (which is unlikely), cluster the ideas and evaluate the value of each cluster, rather than each individual idea.

In the example below, six clusters of solutions were created. While none of the single ideas may be the right one, the clusters allow us to define what direction to explore further as we start creating potential solutions.

How might I make more money without being stressed?

Get more balance

- Meditating
- Become a yoga instructor

Get a better paid job

- Find a job with higher pay and less responsibilities

It's all about people

- Work with my friend Jo

Make my passion pay

- Sell art on Etsy
- Start a side cooking business
- Find a job I really love
- Sell online classes that are evergreen

Get money from others

- Find a rich boyfriend
- Ask family or friends

Increase my value

- Become a consultant
- Get new certifications that help me get higher paying jobs
- Write a book to become famous

▶ Randomly place each note on an easel sheet or virtual board.

▶ Ask the whole group (or a subgroup if the group is too large) to silently cluster the notes. Don't create categories in advance. It's better to see what comes out of the clustering process.

▶ Each person moves a note around and places it with other notes that they think fit together:

- If one participant doesn't agree with the placement, they can move the note back or duplicate it (so that the same idea may end up in two different clusters).

- Don't try to fit every note into a large cluster. Smaller, specific clusters and notes left alone are useful, too.

- You'll usually end up with five to ten clusters.

▶ Once all the clusters are set up (or when you think they're good enough), discuss and name them as a group:

- Be sure the name is more than a label, and that it reflects the essence of the idea.

- Create a title that's interesting and memorable. Think about a book or article headline. In the above example, rather than calling the cluster "Activities," a better name might be, "Make my passion pay."

▶ Finally, vote to determine which clusters you want to move forward (using predetermined criteria or other, more sophisticated tools). Remember to use the criteria you have identified upfront when you vote (see page 77 for example of criteria).

TIP

Clustering silently will save a lot of time and make the clustering process much more efficient. Avoid talking during this phase.

Keys to Success:

- ☑ **Remind the group of the converging rules.**

- ☑ **Create or review criteria for success,** so everyone is evaluating the elements the same way.

- ☑ If you have more than 75–100 ideas to start, vote to **narrow down the ideas first**, then do the clustering/naming/voting exercise. Otherwise, just cluster. In this stage, keep any idea that got at least one vote, as we are early in the process. If someone found that idea interesting, it's worth considering for a little while longer.

- ☑ **Be sure to do the clustering part SILENTLY.** Otherwise it will take forever, as team members will start discussing each placement.

Practice #9:
Brainstorming

Take the problem statement you generated in practice #8, and do a brainstorming, including the diverge and converge part:

Use sticky notes to generate at least 20 ideas on your own, or 100 if you are working with a team.

_____

_____

_____

_____

Then cluster the ideas and create a title for each cluster to summarize the core idea.

_____

_____

_____

_____

Pick one cluster that you would be interested in exploring further.

_____

_____

_____

_____

■ Tools for Developing Options

Prototyping

Prototyping is a great activity to use during this phase, which may include both diverging and converging aspects. Ultimately, prototyping is more than just a tool—it's a mindset. The "prototyping attitude" is emphasized in the work of IDEO. This is how IDEO co-founder Tom Kelley explains the role of a prototype, "A prototype is almost like a spokesperson for a particular point of view, crystallizing the group feedback and keeping things moving."[45]

We can talk about ideas and use words to describe them, but each of us may have a different interpretation of what the concept actually means. Once we start representing that idea concretely, it's much easier to understand it, react to it, and provide feedback.

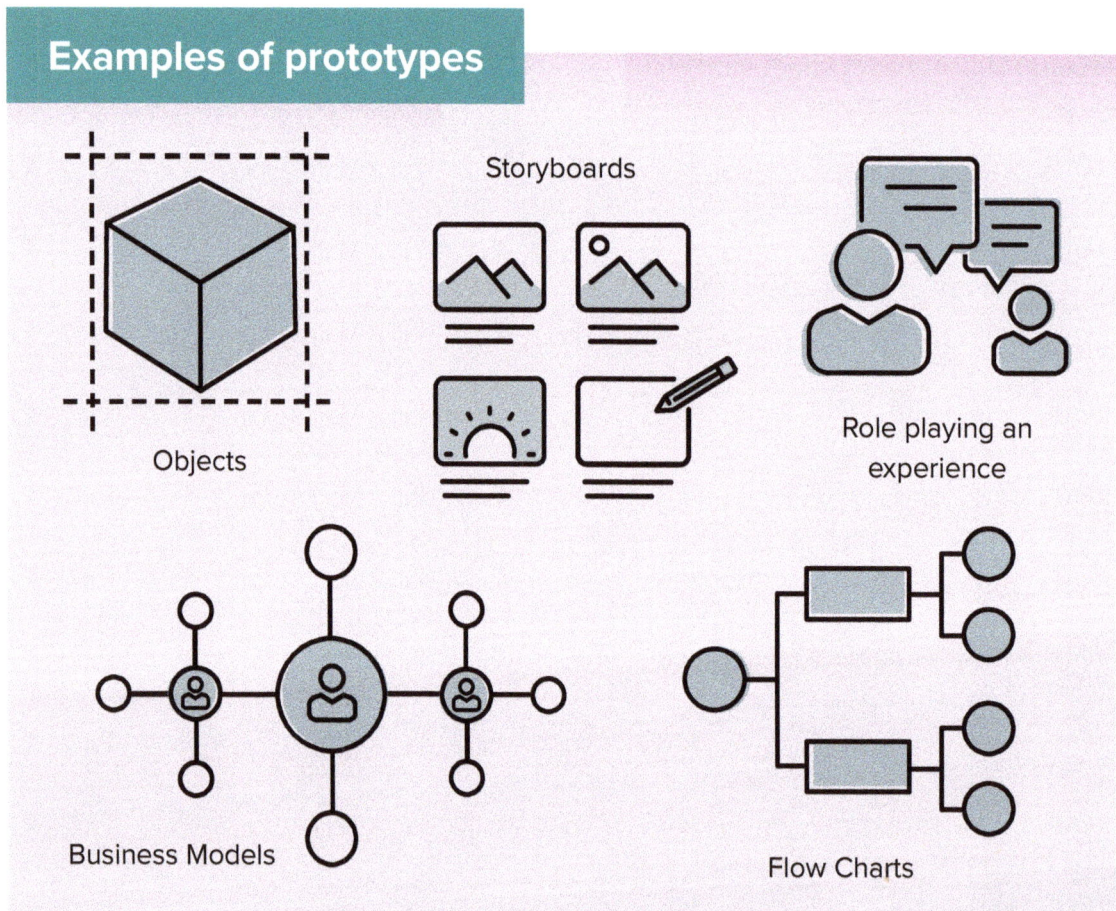

Examples of prototypes

Objects

Storyboards

Role playing an experience

Business Models

Flow Charts

[45]Kelley, T. (with Litman, J.) (2001). *The Art of Innovation*: lessons in creativity from IDEO, America's leading design firm, p. 111. Doubleday.

☑ **Let go of the concept of perfection** (which is often part of the corporate culture). Be willing to share rough ideas, and to ask for and be open to feedback.

☑ *Everything* **can be prototyped.** Not only objects, but services and experiences, too. Find a way to prototype your solutions.

☑ **Start with the roughest version.** Give yourself a limited time (say ten minutes or an hour) and a budget (from no cost to less than $100), and think what you might create under those constraints.

☑ **No need to prototype the whole solution.** Start with the simplest version, or even a part of the solution (sometimes called the Minimum Value Proposition or MVP).

☑ **The rougher, the better.** This may seem counterintuitive, but you're more likely to get useful feedback on a prototype if it looks very rough. People are less intimidated and feel they're providing useful feedback when a prototype looks unfinished. A prototype that looks very polished may limit honest feedback, since people either don't want to hurt the feelings of the person showing it (as they may think a lot of thought has gone into creating it), or they think they may be the only one who doesn't understand why this is the best solution. No one wants to look stupid or critical.

How to create a prototype and get feedback:

1) Think about the best way to represent the idea/solution:

▶ **Drawing.** This could be hand-drawn and it doesn't need to be professional quality. AI can help with the visual, or even generating concepts.

▶ **A 3D representation.** This might be made using art and crafts (I often use Playdo®, aluminum foil, pipe cleaners, strings, or paper), or create a computerized model.

▶ **Flow charts** are a great way to represent systemic or experiential changes.

▶ **Skits** are very helpful to represent an experience.

▶ **Videos** as a great way to show how your product, service or experience may work.

▶ **Collages** can help describe an environment, mood, type of users, context around the idea.

▶ **Scenarios.** For example, describe a customer journey using your new product/service/experience.

▶ **Prototyping in the wild.** The idea here is to find a way to make your prototype visible and "purchasable," as if it has a value (even if it's not really available). The fact that people will try to purchase it and look for information about it helps to gauge interest. It's often what products do on Indiegogo or Kickstarter, when they offer people the ability to purchase a product that's still in its early development stage and may be delivered months later—or even not at all.

2) Create a series of prototypes around your idea (diverge).

3) Get feedback quickly and test to learn:

• Since this is intended to be very small-scale qualitative research, you don't need to worry about representation at first. Ask colleagues, family members, and friends. If you can, ask potential users—perhaps doing this virtually on Zoom.

• Focus on whether the audience understands the prototype and how they may or may not use it in their life. Don't ask for ratings or if they like it (that's not important at this early stage), but rather focus on use and usability.

• If issues come up quickly, modify the prototype to address the issues and continue to iterate as you seek input.

- Iterating rough prototypes doesn't mean taking a lot of time. *For instance, if three people mentioned they can't figure out where to find the power button, you may not need 50 more people to tell you the same thing before you realize you need to make this button more visible.*

4) Iterate, iterate, and iterate before moving to more refined prototypes. Only through iterations can you start fine-tuning your solutions and working towards more relevant prototypes, which can then be refined.

TIP

Get feedback fast

When I work with groups that are developing new ideas and solutions, we sometimes schedule in-person or online one-on-one sessions with users. Over a few hours, the group can get feedback and iterate with 20 to 30 users in a fast and very efficient manner. Asking for feedback individually avoids group biases.

POINt[46]

POINt stands for **Pluses, Opportunities, Issues**, and **New thinking**. This is one of my favorite tools, as it's very versatile and can be used not only to evaluate and develop ideas but also to evaluate meetings and training programs. This is a great way to anticipate issues that may arise from users, stakeholders, partners, finance, manufacturing, etc., and to develop ways to address these concerns before they become problems. In essence, you proactively address potential issues with your new ideas/solutions/prototypes, then decide that they may be solvable, or that this idea/solution/prototype should be disregarded or not prioritized further.

Steps:

On an easel sheet, or using a physical or virtual white board, ask the group to identify:

▶ **Pluses:** What do you (all) like about the idea?

▶ **Opportunities:** What may this idea do in the future for you, your team, your organization, or your users? Because we don't know the future, this is about anticipating the ways this idea may have potential.

▶ **Issues:** List all the issues (a great way to anticipate judgment and idea killers). The trick is to turn all these issues into questions, using statement starters (see the tool above). Then decide to tackle the issues one-by-one or converge and identify the critical concerns.

▶ **New Thinking:** Now that you've identified the issues, it's time to brainstorm ways to solve them by identifying at least five new ideas.

▶ **Evaluate** these ideas and decide what to do next. You've anticipated possible issues and ways to address them, and it's now time to either fine-tune the solution, if you think it still has potential, or decide that it's not worth pursuing further.

---

[46]Source: FourSight®, an earlier version was developed in the 1980s by Diane Foucar-Szocki, Bill Shephard, and Roger Firestien.

POINt about this book after writing my first draft

Pluses: I like

- It addresses innovation challenges from a practical perspective
- It is interactive
- It focused on learning by doing
- It has a personal tone
- It is short

Opportunities: It might

- Be successful
- Be useful to my past or future clients
- Get readers more comfortable with innovation and change
- Provides me some opportunities to speak

Issues: (*selected issues)

- How to be sure it is enjoyable to read?*
- How to make it interactive?*
- How to let people know about the book so they buy want to buy it?
- How to make money from the book?

New Thinking (*selected ideas):

How to be sure it is enjoyable to read?

- Have friends and colleagues read it and provide feedback*
- Have a professional editor read it*
- Share it with a writers' group
- Have a 10-year-old read it

How to make it interactive?

- Include at least a practice per chapter*
- Create a multiweek program where readers can put it all together and see the impact*
- Ask readers to discuss with others (family/peers/team)*
- Have videos of each chapter key take aways
- Create an on-line course
- Create an AI bot that can answer readers' questions

Here's the version of POINt adapted as a tool to evaluate trainings or meetings.

▶ **Pluses:**
- What did we like about the meeting or training session?
- What worked well?
- What did we learn or relearn (for training sessions)?
- What did we accomplish (for meetings)?
- What else did we like?

▶ **Opportunities:**
- What may this learning or meeting do for this team/our organization/our lives?
- How might this have an impact?

▶ **Issues:** What are the issues or concerns that we have related to this meeting/training? Be sure to list these as questions starting with statement starters:
- How to . . . ?
- How might . . . ?
- What might be all the . . . ?
- In what ways might . . . ?

▶ **New Thinking:**
- Select the most important concerns. For each, generate ideas on how to address them.
- Decide which ideas you want to incorporate to address the concerns and which ones will not be selected.

Keys to Success:

☑ Use a diverging mindset to answer the first two questions.

☑ Use a diverge-then-converge mindset for the next two questions.

☑ Do this as a group and encourage discussion.

Implementation: Action Planning[47]

This approach is unique, in that it includes both diverge and converge approaches to creating an action plan. This gives you the opportunity to examine many options for planning to implement your ideas, rather than assuming there's only one single path.

Steps:

▶ Create a chart.

▶ Brainstorm possible actions on sticky notes.

▶ Select actions to be kept.

▶ Determine the short-term, mid-term, and long-term timing of your project. This might be a week, a month, or six months—it's up to you to define.

▶ Organize actions in the order they should be completed.

▶ For each action selected, determine the person and team responsible, the timing for completion, to whom the outcome will be reported, and the type of outcome expected (which helps with accountability).

Keys to Success:

☑ Spend time diverging on possible actions.

☑ Be very clear about accountability, deadlines, and how you'll define completion.

☑ Start at least one action very quickly to keep momentum going.

---

[47]Miller, B., Vehar, J., & Firestien R. (2004). *Creativity unbound: An introduction to creative process (4th Ed.)*. Thinc Communication.

Action	Outcome	By Whom	By When	Reporting To
Short-Term				
Mid-Term				
Long-Term				

48

---

[48]Miller, B., Vehar, J. & Firestein, R. (2004). *Creativity unbound : an introduction to creative process* (4th Ed.) Thinc Communications.

Practice #10:
Action Plan

Solve a challenge using the tools we've discussed by following this template.

1. What challenge am I/are we solving? Or, what opportunities am I exploring?

a. Initial challenge/opportunity: ....

....

b. Diagnostic: What are the questions to consider?

Who ....

What ....

Where ....

When ....

Why ....

How ....

c. If needed, research more data (online for example), and interview/observe others who are dealing with that challenge. Or, you could journal and reflect on your challenge.

....

....

....

2. Based on a better understanding of the situation, what specific problem do I/we actually want to solve? Create a list of possible problems or challenges; then pick one.

....

....

....

3. What ideas do we have to solve the problem? List a number of ideas, then pick one, a combination, or a cluster.

....

....

....

4. How can we create prototypes and test my solutions? List different ways to create prototypes and/or create several, then pick the one(s) for which you want to get feedback or test.

....

....

....

5. If possible, create a prototype and get feedback.

6. How might we implement the solution we choose? List all the possible actions, then select the ones you want to implement. Use the action plan template to include timing, responsibilities, and outcomes. If possible, implement your plan.

....

....

....

Chapter 7

Lighting the Path:
Sustaining Creativity and Innovation

While we have seen incredible changes in the workplace over the last several years, we are just starting on a journey that will likely see more accelerated and dramatic change.

The COVID pandemic affected the entire world simultaneously and transformed the way we work, live, and connect with others. We were reminded that change is inevitable, and that disruption may come quickly. Just when we were relaxing, thinking we may be going back to a somewhat more normal environment, a new generation of generative artificial intelligence (AI) tools was unleashed on the world.

OpenAI released ChatGPT and immediately we took off on a wild ride. While it took 16 years for mobile phones and nine months for TikTok to reach 100 million users, it took ChatGPT two months to get there (and only five days to reach the first million users!).[49]

---

[49]https://economictimes.indiatimes.com/news/new-updates/chatgpt-witnesses-massive-rise-chatbot-gains-100-million-users-in-two-months/articleshow/98428443.cms?from=mdr.

In a world that is transforming at a rapid pace never seen before, creativity and innovation skills are needed even more than ever to help us adapt quickly. Whether we like it or not, there's no going back.

The world of work is very different in this new AI era. The pandemic exposed workplace issues and created changes that are here to stay, but AI is creating changes that we cannot even imagine. My biggest take away from the 2023 TED conference was that no one fully understands how AI Learning Language Models (LLMs) work and are evolving, what they can or cannot do (this is a black box—even for the companies that created them), nor the possible impact. The skills and framework suggested in this book can help individuals and teams better adapt to a faster changing world, while bringing more satisfaction and joy to your personal and work life.

Now, more than ever, we understand that we are looking for connection and meaning in our work and lives. If we don't find it, we'll go somewhere else or simply quit.

Work environments are changing—many people are choosing to continue to work remotely, and smart organizations are creating hybrid environments. We've seen that physical aspects are not as important as we once thought. It turns out many jobs can be handled just as effectively and productively remotely as in person.

The question becomes more important with AI. How do we build and cultivate connections and get a sense for belonging (to a team and an organization), when AI can make us feel even more isolated, providing us answers but lacking humanity? A recent study published by the American Psychological Association shows that employees using AI are feeling more lonely and as a result more likely to be drinking.[50]

> Now, more than ever, we understand that we are looking for connection and meaning in our work and lives. If we don't find it, we'll go somewhere else or simply quit.

---

[50]https://www.apa.org/pubs/journals/releases/apl-apl0001103.pdf.
Tang, P. M., Koopman, J., Mai, K. M., De Cremer, D., Zhang, J. H., Reynders, P., Ng, C. T. S., & Chen, I-H. (2023). No person is an island: Unpacking the work and after-work consequences of interacting with artificial intelligence. *Journal of Applied Psychology*. Advance online publication. https://doi.org/10.1037/apl0001103.

On the positive side, biases may also be less acute on a screen. Some might even go away. Disabled people, or those living in dispersed geographical locations, can now have access to jobs that would have previously been available only in person. People whose job options were limited by transportation issues now have access to more opportunities. As a result, teams may become more diverse in all the dimensions we've described. That's a huge benefit—assuming you are aware of and know how to manage diversity in a team.

While AI can be an enabler to more creativity at a scale never seen before, there's also a negative side. AI can bring new biases we didn't even know exist—as these tools have been trained using the internet, not the best unbiased source. We therefore need to stay vigilant in our understanding and evaluation of potential outcomes of working with AI.

Personal interactions are changing, too. Being together is no longer a given, but more of a conscious decision (sometimes dictated by the employer, sometimes decided by the team members). Assuming there's a choice, a team may ask these questions to help decide the best format for collaboration for each type of meeting:

- **Do we really need to meet?** Sometimes a formal meeting isn't even needed, and work can be done just as effectively asynchronously using a collaboration platform.

- **Do we need to all meet *in person?*** Perhaps remote or hybrid meetings will work as well.

- **What is the right balance for our team?** How do we trade off convenience and speed versus in-person connection?

- **How do we make meetings as worthwhile as possible?** This might include focusing on activities that are harder or impossible to do in person, as well as adding personal connection time (such as lunch, dinner, and team building activities).

Expectations are also changing. The assumptions team members previously had about how they fit in the organization and how their jobs fit into their lives are different now. Employees want to be able to have the flexibility to be there for their children, make necessary appointments, or run errands—without being controlled or needing to ask permission. On the other hand, employees are also more willing to work outside of regular business hours to make up for this flexibility. Ultimately, this is about trust and self-responsibility, and acknowledging that outcomes are more important than the time spent or the specific time of the day an activity is completed.

■ A Virtual, Hybrid World Create New Challenges

Many employees are disengaged.

They don't feel involved with their organization or their team. As a result, in 2022 we saw "The Great Resignation." Thousands of people were leaving their jobs—and, in some cases, leaving the workforce entirely. This trend slowed in 2023, but employees became more aware of what they considered important factors for them to be invested in their job. To enhance innovation, organizations should make sure team members feel they're being seen and heard, and that they have a chance to thrive and use their skills.

It's important to understand why your people may not be engaged. Take time to analyze team meetings, and determine what could be improved. Ask for feedback. What might be missing? In an open discussion format, this can be very powerful. The POINt format is a great tool for this (see page 110). Of course, one-on-one feedback discussions are also important to understand motivations and aspirations. Innovation work may actually be a great avenue for empowerment, since it's about creating something new and challenging the status quo.

The camaraderie is different.

When employees work remotely, there's no break room, coffeemaker, or water cooler to gather around. As a result, employees may feel a lack of community. They can't have the quick, off-the-cuff discussions with fellow workers that often generate innovative ideas and a sense of belonging or co-creation (or commiseration). Some in-person get-togethers are important, as are team activities that are not focused on solving problems, such as training opportunities, working in small groups, or

| TIP | Be aware of team building activities without purpose. |

more possibilities to collaborate on projects or team building activities. On a regular basis, you can introduce small talk, check-ins, temperature checks, one-minute meditation, or other quick activities before jumping into the business part of a meeting. This may help people be more present and bring their whole self to virtual meetings.

Sometimes "team building activities" are considered enough to create goodwill. However, they can have no positive impact, or even have a negative one, if they're not well thought-through. When you plan team building activities, think about these things:

- **Criteria:** Consider whether it's simply getting the team to have fun together, learn something new, communicate better, get to know each other at a personal level, or provide an exhilarating experience. Also think about the criteria that will help with team engagement, such as the best time of the day (during work hours or not—which may be challenging for team members with small children or other personal constraints), length of the meeting, safety and level of comfort (particularly in the post-COVID era), travel requirements, etc.

- **Outcomes:** At the end of the day, what are you trying to accomplish, and how would you know the activity was successful?

- **Debriefing and Taking It Forward:** For team building activities that are more than purely social, think about how you will debrief and move the learning forward to create long-lasting changes. There's nothing worse than promoting something during a team building activity (such as being more vulnerable or thinking outside the box), and then go back the next week and being told or seeing that these principles are not applied within the organization. This creates disappointment and disengagement, which may be worse than not having the team building program in the first place.

Discussing the benefits and learning from an experience together can be more powerful than the experience itself.

In my workshops, I often include improv games, because they're connected to being more creative, staying in the present, having fun, making your partners look good, accepting all the offers, or letting go of your voice of judgment. After we play and have fun, we take time to talk about the games and what was learned, as it relates to creativity and innovation.

Team members have other obligations.

During the pandemic, we realized that family and personal health must come first for team members. This includes both physical and mental health issues—some of which were made worse by COVID. Your team members need to meet their personal obligations. Consider if everyone really needs to be together at one time. If not, work more asynchronously, which allows other people to give input before and after a meeting. Not everything needs to be present in the meeting.

We're missing a dimension.

In a remote environment, it's too easy to miss nonverbal cues. Virtual meeting software is two-dimensional (and, depending on the organizational culture, it can even be one-dimensional, when people don't turn on their camera). People miss the connection to others and the energy that comes from an intense interactive discussion, and from feeling the energy of each person and the room. It's also hard to speak in turn if you're using a platform that can't support simultaneous discussion or back-and-forth conversation. Tools like breakout rooms, white boards, small groups, and better chat rooms can help alleviate some of these issues.

■ A Virtual/Hybrid World Also Offers New and Sometimes Better Solutions

Collaboration is king.

There are great collaborative tools available—and they continue to evolve and improve as time goes on. Take advantage of white boards, polls, and breakout rooms. Integrate interactive discussion and collaboration exercises in small groups into the agenda to create more opportunities for conversation and to improve participation. Consider the right platform (Slack, for example) to facilitate ongoing dialogues and connections. Meetings should not be for presentations (which can be done prior to the meeting). Unstructured discussion is also very inefficient in terms of active participation. At least half of the time in a meeting should be collaboration—not talking or presenting.

It may be easier to be heard.

In this dispersed environment, diverse voices can be heard more easily. No one voice is more valued in a discussion. That means it no longer matters where your office is located or what your title is—everyone can speak up in a virtual meeting. Tools that allow team members to raise their (virtual) hands, round-robin formats, and, of course, breakout rooms can make the process more democratic.

Gathering input has changed.

It's now easier to gather simultaneous input. Everyone has the same opportunity—each is in their own space, no one is in the front or back. Ask team members to raise their hands and take their input in order. With real-time polls, you can also see where the group is at that moment and get results immediately. In addition, the chat box allows everyone to comment at the same time (granted, it may get chaotic or hard to read). White boards are also a great way to get and see all the comments and thoughts in one place and at the same time.

Virtual and hybrid work can be more inclusive.

Everyone can be involved. Before, participating in an innovation team discussion may have involved travel and time away from home. Now, it's easier to include people at remote sites—whether those sites are located next door or around the world. This also helps to more easily include people with disabilities for whom travelling, ergonomics, and the office environment (too much noise, for example) may be challenging.

Managing the new mix.

How will we manage some members working remote and some being present in person? What kind of hybrid situation can we develop to solve team problems and maintain innovation?

Hybrid meetings, where some people are in person and others are online, raise another set of issues. This situation may feel harder to manage than a meeting where everyone is either in the room or virtual.

Here are a few ways to make these meetings more productive:

- If possible, use technology that allows the group in the office to easily see virtual participants (such as projecting the virtual attendees on a large screen monitor).

- Check the technology before the meeting. Too often, a great deal of time is wasted trying to figure out the system and get all virtual participants online.

- Ask virtual participants to be on camera (so they are seen) and, if possible, to keep their sound on (so it's easier for them to speak).

- A facilitator can be particularly useful for these meetings, as they can ensure that virtual participants are fully included and engaged, have the same access to documents, and can be easily heard.

- When creating the agenda and activities, think about the best way to have virtual participants involved. For example, create a breakout room where all the virtual people work together, while the in-person participants meet in real breakout rooms. Or, create groups that mix virtual and in-person attendees.

Always remember to include those people who are virtual and give them the same chance to be seen and heard. That may require extra awareness and effort. If the virtual group is large, you may have somebody monitoring the chat box and/or making sure they have the same "airtime" as the people in the room, as well as dealing with any technical difficulties.

Technology can be our friend—if we understand how to harness it properly. We need to learn how to use new technologies, such as online white boards, and to develop better asynchronous communication. We also need to remember that technology should be here to serve a purpose. Investing in technology for its own sake will not solve problems— in fact, it may create new ones.

> Now, more than ever, we understand that we are looking for connection and meaning in our work and lives. If we don't find it, we'll go somewhere else It's even more important for in-person meetings to be thought through in detail, so that limited time is used as effectively as possible.

A chance to reinvent the way things are done in business.

Sure, we're not going back to the way things were in 2019. Some things have been lost, but there are opportunities, too. We have the chance to reinvent the way things are done in groups and offer better personal life-balance (by not being in the office five days each week). People can work where they want—and they may even relocate to other areas where they'd prefer to live.

In a *Harvard Business Review* article called "The 'Great Resignation' is a Misnomer," Whitney Johnson suggests this should instead be called the "Great Aspiration," as the pandemic has made people realize that life can be short, and that they better find their passion and meaning in their life and their job. The ways we help teams collaborate—appreciating each other, avoiding friction, and being more inclusive—can have an impact on satisfaction and motivation in their jobs, and encourage them to participate fully and remain with the organization.[51]

Today's managers will be tasked with learning how to build engagement in this new world and finding ways to maintain innovation.

Those organizations that are proactive will learn how to make the most of the situation. They'll ask, what advantages can I leverage when implementing remote teams? How can we use technology to best benefit both our people and our business? What pitfalls should we be avoiding? How can I use this new environment to improve satisfaction and fulfillment for my employees and co-workers, both in their jobs and their lives?

---

[51]Johnson, W. (2022). The "Great Resignation" is a misnomer. Harvard Business Review, April 06, 2022. *https://hbr.org/2022/04/the-great-resignation-is-a-misnomer.*

Some executives, like Tesla CEO Elon Musk, may believe that being back in the office full time is the only solution to productivity. This seems backward and wishful thinking that doesn't take into consideration what the biggest virtual experience in the world has taught us about what's possible and desirable for most workers. Many companies have acknowledged that full-time office attendance may not be possible if they want to retain their workforce, nor is this desirable from a financial perspective (office space is expensive, and many organizations have renegotiated their leases or downsized their space). It's not even realistic in a global world where the workforce is dispersed across continents.

The current trend appears to be two to three days at a maximum in the office for most employees whose jobs don't require them to be onsite all the time. Some tech companies, like Cisco and Intel, have acknowledged that they won't require in-person attendance at all for some jobs. This makes time in the office even more precious. It's even more important for in-person meetings to be thought through in detail, so that limited time is used as effectively as possible.

Practice #11:
Managing Hybrid Meetings

Think about your next remote or hybrid meeting and consider how you can help colleagues be more involved and more collaborative.

Create an agenda integrating the following points:

What activities can we include at the beginning and the end of the meeting to create more connections?

....

....

How can we ensure everyone is participating?

....

....

What can be done asynchronously before or after the meeting?

....

....

How will we handle team members who can't attend the meeting?

....

....

After the meeting, create a POINt (see page 110). Even better, do this together with your colleagues at the end of the meeting.

■ The Big Question: How Will AI Impact Our Thinking and Work Around Innovation, Creativity, and Change?

As I put the finishing touches on this book, AI began to totally transform our world. One thing that is certain: moving forward, AI will be part of our innovative process as a way to provide options and input.

The recently published *Manifesto for Collaboration* highlights different scenarios: from a collaboration with AI seen as a tool and possible partner, to giving up and letting AI do all the creative work, to simple plagiarism where attributions and roles are unclear, to making human-only creative endeavor the premium approach.[52]

While all these may happen, depending on the areas where creativity is used, my hope is that we keep a place for collaboration where humans will still play a key part in these key areas:

- Creating the context to define the focus for areas we want to consider for innovation and changes.

- Decision making: AI can suggest and recommend, but ultimately, decisions need to be made and risks taken by human decision makers. As discussed earlier, wicked problems will be created and AI will still be in a state of uncertainty, since innovation will happen in a world in perpetual and arguably faster changes, which create somewhat unpredictable situations.

- Bringing our unique stories and perspectives: As much as AI can analyze data about our lives, we are still the only ones who actually live our lives, feel the emotions, and each go on a unique journey.

---

[52]Vinchon F., Lubart T., Bartolotta S., Gironnay V., Botella M., Bourgeois-Bougrine S., Burkhardt J-M., Bonnardel N., Corazza G.E, Glăveanu V., Hanchett Hanson M., Lvcevic Z., Karwowski M., Kaufman J.C., Okada T., Reiter-Palmon R. and Gaggioli A. (2023). *The Journal of Creative Behavior.* Wiley Periodicals LLC on behalf of Creative Education Foundation (CEF). https://onlinelibrary.wiley.com/doi/epdf/10.1002/jocb.597.

As of 2023, here is an initial framework and questions that may be useful as we navigate these changes:

- **Understanding the basics** of an innovation process is even more important when the content can be co-created or possibly (partially) delegated to AI.

- **Remember key principles:** the importance of defining the problem, having clear criteria, getting user viewpoints, prototyping and testing in real life—no matter how fancy the prediction model may be—and the willingness to fail and iterate. This will allow you to still be in the driving seat of the process rather than just accept the black box of AI suggestions. Rei Inamoto captured this quite succinctly: "AI is quickly taking away from humans the work of generating and even crafting something. So the job that's left for humans is to imagine what magic to create."[53]

At a broader level, there are several elements that may be very important to successful innovation with AI in the future:

- A clear legal framework to understand what is ownable and patentable when working on innovation products/services or experiences.

- A way to identify what is human-created, AI-created or co-created through clear systems (such as a watermark for pictures), so we can distinguish facts and fakes, and real versus invented (granted, the lines are getting quite blurry).

- A way to better understand the "black box," so suggestions from AI can be sourced back and verified.

- A way to use AI in a way that is confidential, so you can share confidential information from your organization that will be critical for innovation. (Right now, the information that you input to ChatGPT is *not* confidential.)

- Clear protection of privacy and data.

- Ability to limit biases and promote fairness.

- Critically, protection against harm to humans, as well as finding ways to ensure that AI has human interest at the core.

[53]Imamoto, R. (2023) . The end of brands as we know them. Medium June 3 https://uxdesign.cc/the-end-of-brands-as-we-know-them-97e8a6480a8.

How Can I Use AI in Innovation Work?

Right now, AI can be a tool to help with the diverging process, such as:

- Looking at trends and summarizing them for background information.
- Summarizing data we have from research.
- Identifying a list of potential problems.
- Identifying ideas for solving problems.
- Illustrating the concepts/new ideas/scenarios around the new solutions.
- Testing concepts with AI-created personas and users (unsure how much I would trust this when dealing with major innovation that cannot rely on the past to predict future behaviors).
- Identifying possible steps to test and implement your solutions.
- Summarizing and analyzing data from testing and failures.

> *"AI is quickly taking away from humans the work of generating and even crafting something. So the job that's left for humans is to imagine what magic to create."*
>
> – Rei Inamoto

I would be very careful at this stage when working on converging activities, beyond suggestions, because of fact that AI is a black box that does not provide sources or rationale for its reasoning. In particular, I would be vigilant around:

- Defining criteria for success.
- Deciding which trends are more important to a team.
- Picking the problem on which the team should work. AI could help quantify the importance of a problem. as long as we give it clearly defined criteria.
- Selecting the ideas to move forward.
- Using AI to predict which new ideas have more chance of success (if it is a really innovative idea)
- Testing with virtual users, rather than human ones—particularly with innovative ideas that require a change in behavior.

- Killing ideas. Remember the converging rule of giving ideas a chance by being deliberate and considering the positive.

I would also be concerned about relying on AI decisions when dealing with team dynamics and human feelings. Having AI make all the decisions is likely to demotivate the team (assuming we still have a team and some human jobs!).

Questions to Ask When Incorporating AI into the Innovation Process

- If everyone or every organization has the same access to AI and its suggestions, how do you differentiate your new ideas?

- Are you ready and willing to trust AI enough to delegate decision making to it?

- How is AI creating more wicked problems in an uncertain future?

- Is innovation more likely to fail in a world with an accelerated pace of change?

- How good is AI at converging?

- Predictions are based on the past. How good is AI at predicting trends and future success when innovating?

- AI doesn't have feelings (at least, not yet!). How can it take into consideration human emotions?

- How can you challenge assumptions when you don't know how AI thinks and learns?

- How do you deal with the "not knowing," a key part of innovation, if AI always has an answer?

- How will you know the AI agenda?

- How is AI changing team dynamics?

- How is AI changing your decision-making process?

- Is AI removing the role of intuition in your work?

Practice #12:
Take a Challenge Through AI

Explore AI tools of your choice and use them to go through the innovation process:

Identity a problem.

....

Come up with ideas and narrow them down to a few possibilities.

....

....

Develop prototypes, then review the pros and cons.

....

....

Test with a few people.

Refine your prototype and develop an action plan.

Reflect:

What works?

....

What doesn't work so well?

....

How might you integrate AI in your innovation work in the future?

....

How is AI going to change the work we do in creativity?

As mentioned above, AI is going to be particularly useful for divergent thinking. An AI tool can be a partner that gives you options. This might be gathering existing data and providing options for analyzing it, identifying a series of problems that you might want to solve, generating different ideas, or creating pictures to illustrate concepts. AI may also be useful at providing pros and cons.

However, when it comes to giving numbers, it really depends on what idea you're testing. If you are looking for a tweak on something that already exists, the models are likely to be helpful. However, when something is fundamentally new and different and requires a change of behaviors, the predictability is going to be much harder. For example, while AI may give us new ideas for the next generation iPhone, would AI have created the concept of an iPhone if it didn't already exist? Would AI have been able to predict Airbnb or Uber and Lyft? Would AI realize people would be open to having strangers stay in their homes for days at a time—or trusting a total stranger who is not a professional to drive you from point A to point B?

We also need to continue testing creative hypotheses with real people. Yes, we have technology that you can test with personas, and AI can create virtual users, but if you really are looking for disruptive innovation, testing with virtual users may not be a good predictor, since AI is trained on past behaviors and we are looking for how behavior might change with the disruption.

In the best possible scenario, AI will support innovation work and possibly be a co-creator. I still believe that understanding the fundamental concepts around creativity, innovation, and change, and the key process and steps for innovation will be critical. Consider this: If you just write a short probe asking an AI tool to create a new product or business and you don't understand all the steps, then you may not realize what is missing and neither will the AI tool. If your probe is vague or a bit off-track, the response will be too.

It's even more important to fully understand convergence and evaluation. Delegating convergence to AI without control would mean that we as humans would delegate risks and their consequences, while we—people—are the one being impacted. Innovation ultimately has an impact on people and human systems, which means humans should keep having a say in these decisions.

AI may eventually become integrated in some of the tools described in this book, but I believe the fundamentals of this book will still remain extremely relevant. We are building houses differently than we did 500 years ago, but key architecture principles are still the same. This book was designed to be more about building houses of innovation, rather than educating you about the latest tools of the trade.

A final thought

Right now, much AI technology is open source and not protected. Whatever you generate through an AI tool would be easily recreated or copied by others. Copyright and patent law around AI is mostly inexistent so far.

The issue of competition becomes more critical. We discussed the concept of wicked problems. Given the pace of change, it's possible that we are entering an era of higher unpredictability. This becomes like a chess game where all the pieces are moving at the same time, while the structures that existed for stabilizing the game are becoming obsolete and new ones have not yet been created. These new structures may include regulation, law, politics, rules of war, and engagement, as well as rethinking the work-for-paycheck model.

No matter how we use AI for prediction, human factors will continue to be important. As you are incorporating AI in your innovation practice, consider not only the outcome of the process but also the impact of using AI with your innovation team: Will the use of AI energize or demotivate your team? Is your team feeling their job can be done better by AI? Are they ready to give up that part of their job (which may arguably be the most exciting part) and delegate innovation out? Are you prepared for what might happen if knowledge workers say no and leave in droves?

I believe that creativity is the last frontier in what makes us human and life exciting. Does losing the creative part of a job make us depressed? Will taking refuge in a more artificial world (including augmented reality and customized entertainment created by AI, feeding us what we think we want) stunt our growth and development? Or, to the contrary, will this give us a chance to live a much fuller life with greater capacity for growth and free time (since jobs will be delegated to AI)?

None of us has the answers to these questions. Right now, what's important is just that they are being asked and considered. I hope this book will give you enough framework and understanding of the core principles of innovation that you will be able to actually navigate and be more comfortable in this ever-changing world.

Chapter 8

Fanning the Flames:
Where Do We Go From Here?

Now that you've learned the importance of diverse thinking and some of the underlying principles, process, and tools related to innovation, what should you do next?

■ Key Points Review

Think more broadly and with more empathy.

- Don't make **assumptions** about your team or a problem, without checking them out.

- Try to **understand** how and why people think differently.

- Have **empathy** for people who think differently than you do.

- Ask **questions** to understand how people think and where they get their positions.

- **Observe** what happens in the workplace. Try to understand how backgrounds and experiences influence how individuals think and act.

- **Listen to** each other. Find out what's not working and why. Consider how you can listen better.

Have clear processes.

- Use **diverge-converge** when you're working on solving problems—even by yourself. Take time to suspend judgment and generate options, then come back and sort through the various options. Consider how to select options in a systematic and thoughtful way. And remember: It always takes twice as long to converge as it does to diverge.

> **Remember:**
> **It always takes twice as long to converge as it does to diverge.**

- Have **clear criteria** for success. What does it mean for this team to be successful?

Put people first.

- Put people in positions that use their **strengths and abilities**. People can lead based on what they like, enjoy, or what makes them excited.

- Take the temperature of the organization. Find out what you can do to get and keep people **engaged**.

- Read the **energy** of the room. If people are tired, it's time to take a break. Switch to different activities or get a read on the room.

- Understand **the ideal size group** for effective discussions. In a physical room, seven to nine people is the maximum size of a group to work together efficiently. In a virtual environment, that drops to five people. If more than that are involved, use breakout rooms to create smaller groups that can report back to the overall group later.

- Use **the power of a larger group** to do work in parallel or to split the tasks to allow everyone to contribute and make the process more efficient.

Be more effective.

- **Manage time** effectively. Ask if a meeting is really necessary. If so, who should be in the room (virtually or in person)?

- Think about how to **be efficient**—not necessarily just in meetings. Use online white boards, where people are working in parallel. Give everyone a chance to say what's on their mind so they feel seen, heard, and engaged.

- Get **feedback**. If you don't ask, you won't know. Consider how to build feedback about both the content (what outcomes have we reached?) and the process (how are we collaborating together?). Ask how well the team works together. Without feedback, you'll see the same issues happen again and again, which will likely result in inefficiencies and disengagement.

- Create "**parking lots**"—these are places (flip charts, a specific area on a white board, or a different document) for things that are important but off-topic, so no content is lost, yet the meeting can focus on what is required.

> **Without feedback, you'll see the same issues happen again and again, which will likely result in inefficiencies and disengagement.**

- **Be clear on the decision process.** Understand how decisions are made. Who is the decision maker? Is it the team? The manager? Are the decision makers in the room or not? Understand what works most effectively in your decision-making process.

- **Create clear criteria** upfront and revise during the project, should new elements arise. Be clear that decisions should be made based on established criteria, rather than what people do or don't like.

- **Don't work in a bubble.** Break silos, and think about ways your team can be diverse.

- Remember to **check with your users** to avoid group thinking bias.

Prepare, plan, and improvise.

- If you facilitate the meeting, set up a detailed and outcome-oriented agenda.

- If you work on innovation projects that require a series of meetings, think about what needs to happen (process) and when, as well as the best ways to keep people involved.

- Create detailed outlines and timelines of each session.

- As an outside professional facilitator, my preparation time may run from half the time of a session up to two to three times as long as the actual session.

- Build plenty of time to prepare. As an outside professional faciltator, my preparation time may require up to five times longer than the meeting or workshop itself. If you are an internal facilitator, be sure to build time to prepare and send the agenda prior to the work sessions.

- Be flexible when things actually don't go as planned and you need to make changes on the spot.

How to take this further? We can help.

You've read and completed at least some of the exercises in this book. Hopefully, you have tried to implement some of the tools mentioned in Chapters 5 and 6. So what's next and how might we be of help?

- Take the **Five-Week Innovation Challenge** found in Chapter 9 using the QR code below to download your journal so you can write in directly and journal your answers.

- If you're curious, **schedule a FourSight® session** with us, and learn about your individual profile. Use the QR code below.

- Contact us for a **free consultation** to see how we may help you and your team with your innovation challenges. All our work is customized. We start by understanding the unique innovation profile of individuals and teams using FourSight®. We then develop a training plan and coaching process and identify tools that would best benefit your team. We can also help facilitate a key challenge, so you and your team can best focus on creating meaningful innovative outcomes.

- Consider a customized **Team Innovation Challenge**. We can create a unique experience for your team to help you solve a challenge in a six-week time period, either self-guided or with coaching support.

- Check our **exclusive offers** for our readers, such as tips, quizzes, webinars or events by checking our Readers Club page using the QR code below.

Practice #13:
Post-Journey Assessment: What is/ are your biggest challenge(s)?

Answer these as quickly as possible.

My biggest challenge(s) right now is/are ....
....

I feel stuck ....

I wish I had a magic wand that could ....

So that I could feel ....

What I need to help me think through this challenge is ....
....

I think I can solve this challenge by ....

Here are the tools I now know how to use ....
....

What I learned from reading and using this book is ....
....

Here's what I will start doing ....
....

Here's what I will stop doing or do less of ....

Here's what I will continue doing ....

In the next week, I commit to ....

The key obstacles I see for myself are ....

Here's how I plan to overcome them ....

....

Action Plan: What are you committing to do?

In the next 24 hours, I commit to ....

....

In the next week, I commit to ....

....

In the next one to three months, I commit to ....

....

I will know I am successful, when ....

....

....

....

Chapter 9

Getting Fired Up:
The Five-Week Innovation Challenge

This challenge is designed to help you become more innovative by finding new perspectives, building awareness about your way of thinking, and improving interactions with others as we help you consciously start adopting new practices.

There are five modules. Plan to complete one module per week. Try to do one activity each day for five days each week. The other two days are for incubation and allowing your brain to make new connections.

Spend at least five minutes per day journaling. This will give you a chance to reflect, which is at least as important as the activities themselves.

Download your complimentary copy
of this journal using the QR code. ⟶

Each week will have a different focus:

Week 1: You

Week 2: You and another person

Week 3: You and the team

Week 4: You and those you can impact

Week 5: Putting it all together

Download your complimentary copy of this journal using the QR code on page 143.

Week 1: YOU

This week, you will focus on your own innovation and creativity:

▶ **Expand your perspective:** Identify at least three things you've never done before (diverge), and try at least one of them this week. This could be a class, a new sport, a leisure activity, a new food, a type of diet, or something else.

▶ **Expand your thinking:** Ask *why* at least three times about the same challenge/new idea/ decision. Notice what happens.

▶ **Change your perspective:** For one day, change your routine. Take a different route when driving, sit at a different place at the table, choose a different time to wake up or to conduct regular activities.

▶ **Observe your thinking:** For at least one interaction each day, notice how you solve problems by yourself. Observe how you think and what steps you take.

▶ **Journal:** Each day, take five minutes to journal your thoughts, In particular, write down:

  - Things I have done differently today.

  - How do I feel when I do things differently? What did I notice about the way I think?

At the end of the week, complete the following:

I really enjoyed doing _____ this week.

When I do things differently, I feel _____

It was hard to _____

I felt good overcoming _____

As a result, I feel _____

I started noticing that I tend to solve problems by _____

Sometimes, I get frustrated with myself when I _____

I also get frustrated with others when they _____

One thing I learned this week is _____

What I want to do less or stop doing is _____

What I want to do more is _____

Week 2: YOU and ANOTHER PERSON

This week you'll focus on how you interact and engage with others:

▶ **Expand your perspective:** At least once this week, do something new with someone else. Notice what you learned and how it makes you feel. Ideally, talk about it with the other person and get their perspective.

▶ **Expand your thinking:** Ask yourself who else can help you solve a problem (diverge). Talk to someone with whom you normally would not engage on this—your child, a friend, a colleague. Make a list of possible choices, then pick one and ask that person for help. Notice how different it can feel to involve someone else.

▶ **Change your perspective:** Have a random discussion with a stranger or someone to whom you don't normally talk. How did this bring new insights or perspectives?

▶ **Observe your thinking:** For at least one interaction a day, notice how you go about solving problems with others. Pay attention to how you think, how they think, and how you interact together.

▶ **Journal:** Each day, take five minutes to journal your thoughts. In particular, write down:

  - Things I have done differently today.

  - How do I feel when I do things differently?

  - What did I notice about the way I think?

  - How is my way of thinking different from others?

  - How does this affect me?

At the end of the week, complete the following:

I really enjoyed doing _____ this week.

When I do things differently, I feel _____

Working with somebody else this week made me realize _____

_____

It was hard to _____

I felt good overcoming _____

As a result, I feel _____

I tend to solve problems by _____

I notice others may solve problems differently by _____

Sometimes, I get frustrated with myself when I _____

I get frustrated with others when they _____

One thing I learned this week is _____

What I want to do less or stop doing is _____

What I want to do more is _____

Week 3: YOU and YOUR TEAM

This week, the focus is how you work together with your team:

▶ **Expand your team's perspective:** Suggest and do one thing differently with the team with whom you work. This could be holding shorter meetings, using a different format for getting together in person, starting meetings with a personal check-in, or adding a fun activity to a Zoom meeting.

If you don't work with a team, do the exercise with your family, a group of friends, or a community with which you may be engaged.

▶ **Expand your team thinking:** Use a virtual white board to collaborate. Check Mural (https://www.mural.co/), Miro (https://miro.com/), or even consider using the white board function in Zoom (https://explore.zoom.us/en/products/online-whiteboard/).

▶ **Get feedback from the team:** Use the POINt tool to get feedback about a meeting or an idea. Do this together. The open discussion is the most important part of the exercise.

▶ **Observe the thinking:** Pay attention to an interaction between you and several team members. What works well and what doesn't? When are you collaborating well? When do you feel or hear tension?

▶ **Journal:** Each day, take five minutes to journal your thoughts. In particular, write down:

- Things either I or the team have done differently today.

- How do I feel when things are done differently?

- What did I notice about the way I think and the way other people on the team think?

- How is my way of thinking different from others?

- How does this affect me?

At the end of the week, complete the following:

I really enjoyed doing _____ this week.

When I do things differently, I feel _____

It was hard to _____

I felt good overcoming _____

What seemed to work well as a team was _____

What felt really challenging as a team was _____

What I did to help the team was _____

The impact was _____

One thing I learned this week is _____

What I want to do less or stop doing is _____

What I want to do more is _____

Week 4: YOU and THOSE YOU CAN IMPACT

This week, you'll take a broader perspective—looking at those who you can impact with your actions.

▶ **Expand your perspective:** Do one new thing that may have an impact on your community, such as volunteering for a cause, taking political action, or helping others.

▶ **Change your perspective:** Research a topic of interest that is impacting your community. Think of how you can take action to help.

▶ **Observe your thinking:** Notice how using an innovation mindset in your community makes you feel. How can your innovation skills be of service?

▶ **Change your thinking:** Move from "I'm not sure how I can have an impact in the world on an issue I really care about," to "What might be all the ways I can have an impact?" Choose one issue, and follow the process to see how you can make this happen.

▶ **Journal:** Each day, take five minutes to journal your thoughts. In particular, write down:

- Things I have done differently today.

- How do I feel when I do things differently?

- What did I notice about the way I can contribute to making a difference in the world?

- How is my way of thinking helping me make a difference? What are my gifts?

At the end of the week, complete the following:

I really enjoyed doing _____ this week.

When I do things differently, I feel _____

It was hard to _____

I felt good overcoming _____

As a result, I feel _____

What I learned about my way of thinking and taking action is _____

_____

One thing I learned this week is _____

What I want to do less or stop doing is _____

What I want to do more is _____

Week 5: PUTTING IT ALL TOGETHER

This week is a little different, as we will be focusing on applying the skills you learned to innovate and create change in your personal life, work life, or communities and causes you care about:

Choose one specific project. Refer to the tools in Chapter 5 if necessary. Use AI tools as you see fit. This can be done individually, but is best done with a team.

IMPORTANT: DO THIS IN ONE WEEK. Take a just-do-it attitude, which will help you let go of the need to achieve perfection:

▶ **Identify a challenge.** Write down all you/the team know about this issue. Ask questions and perspectives from others. Do research, interview, or observe people, and identify at least three insights you gain from this process.

▶ **Write down the question you want to solve.** Use the statement starters to generate at least three to ten questions. Choose the challenge that is most relevant, yet not too broad or overwhelming, so that you can work on it quickly.

▶ **Define your criteria for success.** Be clear about how you will measure the results of your effort.

▶ **Ideate:** Go through a divergent exercise to identify at least 30 ideas (ideally at least 50–100 ideas) to solve the challenge, then pick one or two you/the team would like to try. You could also combine ideas or cluster them, then use a cluster of ideas that can then be refined and combined.

▶ **Prototype:** Identify at least two ways to prototype the idea. Draw it, create a story, develop a flow chart, write a skit, or produce a short video. Share these prototypes with at least two people not involved on the project for feedback. Iterate and change, if necessary, based on the feedback. Use POINt to evaluate one, and decide which solution(s) you may consider moving forward.

▶ **Action planning:** Create a plan for how you/the team can continue moving your solution forward. Be sure to *diverge* on the different actions before converging, and identify the ones you/the team will choose to actually take.

Action	Outcome	By Whom	By When	Reporting To
Short-Term				
Mid-Term				
Long-Term				

54

54Ibid.

At the end of this final week, complete the following exercise individually or as a team:

Three things I learned from reading this book.

_____

_____

_____

How might reading and using this book impact what I do in the future?

For me _____

For my life _____

For my family _____

For my professional career _____

For my community _____

For the world _____

What issues or questions does this book raise for me? Remember to phrase the issue as a question (think Jeopardy!).

Use statement starters such as:
How to . . . ? How might . . . ? In what ways might this . . . ?
What might be all the . . . ?

▶ **New Thinking:** Choose a few key issues you've identified. For each, ideate on ways to overcome the challenges. Then select one or two of these possible solutions and move them forward.

Congratulations, Innovator!

By being willing to experiment, reflect and learn, you're likely to change the way you operate in the world. Once you see this, there's no going back!

I hope you will share your experience with others. If this book has been useful to you, please review and recommend to your friends, colleagues and within your organization. And if you would like to get more tips, invitations to special events and webinars, use the QR code below to join our readers club.

Acknowledgments

This book represents my COVID baby—an ambitious challenge I set for myself.

While the idea of writing a book had been on my mind for quite some time, I never truly believed I would take the plunge. The journey began 15 years ago with a conversation with Deborah Clifford, my roommate during my master's studies. We joked about creating a book that would "make creative problem solving sexy." This shared notion became the seed from which this book sprouted. Its fruition, however, was only possible through collaborative efforts.

I extend my heartfelt recognition and gratitude to all the contributors who have touched my life and lent their support to this endeavor.

A special and resounding acknowledgment goes out to my steadfast editor, Linda Popky, whose guidance and persistence steered me through the two-year process of writing this book. Throughout, her encouragement never wavered. During his tenure as the Executive Director of the d.school at Stanford, George Kembel shared his belief that "feedback is a gift." Indeed, these gifts of insight made this book possible. I also want to extend my appreciation to the early readers and reviewers who provided invaluable feedback on the initial version of this book:

Corinne Dive-Reclus, a longtime friend, shared her perspective as an executive with extensive experience in managing large teams. Her encouragement to be concise while staying on point proved invaluable.

My friend David Glover, an author, emboldened me to take on this writing journey. His candid and comprehensive feedback, devoid of sugar coating, propelled the project forward. His analytical PhD mindset ensured that claims were substantiated by research, distinct from my personal perspective.

John Schwab, with whom I have collaborated for years, posed probing questions and provided practical insights that compelled me to delve deeper and refine further.

Stan Hou, a former client turned friend, emphasized the importance of practicality and brevity, urging me to distill key points effectively.

Deborah Clifford, the catalyst behind the "sexy" book conversation years ago, encouraged me to focus on an experiential and practical approach and reassured me that I was on the right course.

Jamie Wheal, whose guidance in the FGP Guide Program strengthened my leadership and my courage to get out of my comfort zone and inspires me to value and create communities and keep expanding to be a full grown human.

My assistant, Jane Wilson, meticulously managed the launch details, contributing significantly to the project's success.

Tina LoSasso for sharing her knowledge and experience about launching a business book.

To all those who dedicated their time to review and provide feedback on this book, your contribution is deeply valued.

I want to share my appreciation to Noah Ray for his beautiful portraits and his talent for capturing my essence and to Holly Barimah for the beautiful graphics that enhance the book and allow me to better share my knowledge visually.

Lastly, none of this would have been possible without the support and love of my children, who supported and encouraged me.

To each of you who has accompanied me on this journey—offering support, insights, and motivation—I am deeply grateful.

About the Author

Photography by Noah Ray

Helene Cahen, M.S., is an innovation consultant, trainer, facilitator, and speaker with over 20 years of experience helping companies navigate innovation challenges. She is the founder and principal consultant at Fire Up Innovation Consulting (previously Strategic Insights), where she guides Fortune 500 companies, small businesses, and non-profits to understand innovation, create innovative new products/services, build effective teams, and support a user-centered culture.

Helene has been a facilitator, coach, and lecturer for the Haas School of Business, and vice president of innovation for a startup. She is in demand as a speaker on the topic of design thinking and creativity, and recently did a TEDx talk on high performance collaboration for teams.

Trained in creative problem solving and design thinking, Helene received an M.S. in Creativity and Change Leadership from the Center for Applied Imagination at the State University of New York (SUNY) Buffalo. She also has a business degree from Sciences-Po Paris, a top French Business School.

Born and raised in Paris, Helene lives in Berkeley, California, with her family. She raised three children and in her spare time is a hiker, an improviser, and a meditator. She recently took up rock climbing to challenge her fear of heights.

www.ingramcontent.com/pod-product-compliance
Lightning Source LLC
Chambersburg PA
CBHW052338210326
41597CB00031B/5291